Selected Scottish Poems for Analysis and Discussion

by

Maureen Brown

With
suggested study points,
revision guides for each poem,
exercises in textual analysis,
critical essay questions
and
suggestions for writing.

ISBN 0 7169 3235 0
© *M. Brown, 1999.*

ROBERT GIBSON · Publisher
17 Fitzroy Place, Glasgow, G3 7SF.

INTRODUCTION

This book is designed to "kill several birds with one stone". It should help you to prepare critical essays for internal assessment and to practise for the critical essay part of the examination at the end of your Higher Still course. All of the poems in the book are Scottish, to take account of the new requirement that at least one of the texts studied must be a Scottish text. You will also have to prepare for the Unseen Textual Analysis part of the exam: there are textual analysis exercises at two levels in each chapter, to help you become familiar with the kinds of questions you will encounter in the examination, as well as the techniques required to answer them. If you are using the book in class, your teacher / lecturer will direct you. You may, however, like to use it for extra independent / supported study. If you are working on your own, start with the exercises at the lower level until you get the hang of it.

Preparing for the English exam

Because English is not a body of knowledge to be learned, people often think there is not much to be done in preparation for the exam. In fact, there is much to revise for all parts of the examination but there is no doubt that the Literary Study Unit is the one which lends itself most to revision. The first requirement is to **know your text well**. You should aim to find something in each poem for yourself. Do not simply swallow the teacher's view of the poem; see if you can add to it with your own observations. Far from being insulted, your teacher will be delighted to see you attempting to make a genuine personal response to the poem. Look for other poems by the same poet: you will be surprised how much light can be shed on the poem you are studying, simply by spotting the same techniques used in a different context, or the same themes being treated with a slightly different slant.

Why poetry?

Perhaps the most convincing argument for some users of this book would be that poems tend to be quite short! Although poems do not take long to read — the shortest in this book is only 12 lines long — they do provide something of a challenge, mainly because poets use language in a condensed form, often at different levels. On the positive side though, it is possible to gain insight into many different social problems or different angles of the same problem from reading one or two poems, as opposed to reading several novels. Sometimes young people are so concerned with their future prospects that they are unwilling to study anything which will not help them directly to get a job. If you are still unconvinced about the merits of studying poetry, I would ask you to stop and consider this: the best poets tend to be particularly sensitive to the human condition. By studying the poet's work, we can benefit from his / her ideas and experiences, which will help us to understand our fellow-human beings and ourselves. What could be more useful to you than that?

CONTENTS

Contents (cont'd)

Contents (cont'd)

HOW TO USE THIS BOOK

Each chapter features a different poet and begins with a note about the poet and his / her work to show both in their contemporary social context. These notes are particularly relevant to the poems included in the chapter, so it may sometimes help to look back at them before / during / after working on the poem.

Suggested Study Points

All chapters contain two poems (three for Burns), accompanied by Suggested Study Points in the form of questions for discussion or just to think about on your own. On the principle that "two heads are better than one", you will probably gain more from this book if you work with a friend or classmate; if, however, you prefer to work on your own, I would advise you to make detailed notes while working through each poem, in order to clarify your thoughts. Your notes will be easier to use if you include the section headings from the book, with words in **bold** type as sub-headings.

The Suggested Study Points are broken up into three sections: **Understanding**, **Analysis** and **Evaluation**. You will be familiar with those terms from your classwork but it is perhaps worthwhile taking a little time to consider what is expected from you in each of those sections.

The questions in the **Understanding** section will lead you to discover:
(a)   what the poem is about, at least superficially — what happens in the poem;
(b)   the poet's viewpoint — is he speaking as himself or through a persona?
(c)   the poet's attitude to his subject;
(d)   the broad theme(s) of the poem.

If you have not understood the points in *(a)* to *(d)* above, then you should read the poem again, with those points in mind, before going on to the Analysis section.

The questions in the **Analysis** section will help you to understand how the poet has achieved his purpose, i.e., how he has managed to put across his theme(s). You will be asked to look at:
(a)   lexical choice — the words he chooses to create particular effects;
(b)   tone — which will tell you the poet's feelings about his subject;
(c)   mood — how the poet makes you feel when you read the poem;
(d)   techniques / devices used to achieve *(b)* and *(c)* above, and to put across his theme(s).

When you have looked closely at individual sections of the poem, you are ready for **Looking over the whole poem**. In this section, you will be directed to consider the effects of features, which affect the overall impact of the poem, such as:
(a)   the poetic form — regular or free verse, rhyme, metre, etc.;
(b)   the literary form — i.e., genre, such as dramatic monologue, sonnet, etc.;
(c)   the title — what light, if any, does it throw on the meaning of the poem?
(d)   the style — e.g., stream of consciousness, irony, humour, etc.;
(e)   the register — e.g., formal, Biblical, etc;
(f)   any other feature which encompasses the whole poem.

In the final section, **Evaluation**, you will be asked to evaluate different aspects of the poem. You would not normally be asked to spend time on a poem, which did not have considerable merit, so you are not being invited to say whether or not this is a good poem. What you will be expected to consider is your personal response to the poem and to the ideas in it. You will be asked to think about:
(a)   the extent to which you agree or disagree with the poet's ideas;
(b)   how effectively the poet has conveyed those ideas to you;
(c)   techniques / devices that you found particularly effective;
(d)   the relevance of the ideas in the poem to your own life;
(e)   whether the poem has confirmed or contradicted ideas you already had; or has led you to think about some aspect of life for the first time or in a new way.

Using Your Notes for Revision

The Suggested Study Points for each poem are followed by revision guides at two levels: Using Your Notes for Revision. This is an opportunity for you to look over your notes to find lines of argument or development, and to discover how individual features work together to give you a more complete overall view of the poem. There are prompts at some of the questions to enable you to check that your notes cover all the important features of the poem. When you have revised your notes, you are invited to practise for the exam by writing an answer to a 10-mark Evaluation question.

Critical Response Guide

The revision guides are followed by a Critical Response Guide for Intermediate 1 and Access 3 levels. These guides will help you to structure your critical response for internal assessment and to flesh out your essay, paragraph by paragraph. Don't forget to refer back to your notes for details and textual references.

Unseen Textual Analysis Exercises

After the work for the two poems, there is a third poem by the same poet, accompanied by Unseen Textual Analysis Exercises at two levels. These exercises will help you to learn the techniques necessary for the Unseen Textual Analysis in the exam. The poems have been chosen because they feature themes or techniques commonly found in the work of each poet; some of these you will already have discussed in the earlier poems in the chapter. You may, of course, use the unseen poems in chapters, which you have not studied, for further exam practice.

Suggestions for Critical Essays and Some Ideas and Suggestions for Writing

At the end of each chapter are Suggestions for Critical Essays and Some Ideas and Suggestions for Writing. Your teacher / lecturer may or may not use the Writing ideas but if you find a particular poem has led you to think more deeply about some experience or aspect of life which interests or affects you personally, you should put those reflections to good use in a piece of Personal Reflective writing. You can never have too much practice or too many pieces to choose from when you come to assemble your Folio, and a piece which has meant something to you is sure to have better ideas, to be more fully developed and to be better expressed than any other. You could also use some of those ideas for your **Individual Oral Presentation**.

Some Useful Definitions

After Chapter 8, there is a section called Some Useful Definitions. Each term is cross-referenced to an example, some of which are worked out for you in the Suggested Study Points, to remind you of the device and its effects. Especially at Higher and Intermediate 2 levels, you can gain "Brownie points" by using those terms in your critical essays as well as in your unseen textual analysis answers . . . *but only if you understand and are able to explain their effects / impact on the poem.*

General Writing Guides

Finally, there are two general writing guides. **Writing Critical Essays** will help you plan, structure and write your critical essays and gives you important information about the requirements in terms of length and criteria for marking these pieces. You will find the three headings, with which you have become familiar in the Suggested Study Points, feature also in the critical essay, with an additional category of Expression. **Writing Essays for the Language Study Unit** will help you with your folio writing. After outlining the requirements, this guide works through the various genres with advice on how to meet the criteria and what the examiner will be looking for in your essay.

Whichever way you use this book, on your own, with a friend, or in class, I hope it will help you in your Higher Still course. Good luck!

Their hooves like pistons in an ancient mill
Move up and down, yet seem as standing still.

Their conquering hooves which trod the stubble down
Were ritual that turned the field to brown,
And their great hulks were seraphim of gold,
Or mute ecstatic monsters on the mould.

from *Horses*, by Edwin Muir, page 66

The picture, by Angela Catlin, shows Brutus, Scotland's largest Clydesdale, beside Heavy Horse, a sculpture at Glasgow Business Park, adjacent to the M8 at Easterhouse, to publicise the first national show and sale of the Clydesdale Horse Society at Stirling Auction Mart on 3rd April, 1998.

CHAPTER 1
Robert Burns:

To a Mouse, Welcome to a Bastart Wean and *Holy Willie's Prayer*

ROBERT BURNS, 1759–1796

The poet and his work

Robert Burns was born on 25th January, 1759, in a clay cottage, which his father had built with his own hands, at Alloway in Ayrshire. He was the first child of William Burnes, gardener, son of a tenant farmer, and Agnes Broun, daughter of a tenant farmer. Burns's birthday is celebrated throughout the world with Burns Suppers, the main dish being haggis, champit tatties and bashed neeps — an attempt to replicate the standard fare of his time — though nowadays the haggis dish is sometimes relegated to the starter and we even have vegetarian haggis!

Burns is often portrayed as an ignorant ploughman but he was nothing of the sort; he was better educated than most ordinary people, of his own time as well as of today. His father, though poor, contrived to have his sons taught to read and write in English, studying classics such as Shakespeare and all of the major writers of his time, and even learning a little French.

By the age of 15, Robert had to work on the farm, where he fell in love with a 14 year old girl, who was the inspiration for his first attempt at verse:

> 'Tis this in Nelly pleases me,
> 'Tis this enchants my soul;
> For absolutely in my breast
> She reigns without controul.

"Shows the ability to do better," his teacher might have written! But, like his first attempt, all of his best poetry comes from his heart: not only the great love songs like *A Red, Red Rose* and *Ae Fond Kiss* but also the poems which deal with the plight of the poor, like the peasant farmers in his community, and the oppressed throughout the world. He had a genuine love for his fellow men: *Auld Lang Syne* has become the world-wide anthem of friendship; and he hated vanity and hypocrisy — particularly that of the Calvinist religion which had a great deal of control over the lives of ordinary folk.

Burns's first volume of poems was published in Kilmarnock in 1786, following which he was taken up by the literati and high society in Edinburgh, who, however, put him on the wrong track by persuading him to write in "proper English", the language of educated people: those poems are amongst his least successful, being somewhat derivative and far removed from his own voice. Thankfully, he soon returned to his own language.

After farming unsuccessfully at Ellisland, near Dumfries, he became an Excise officer and lived in the town of Dumfries, where he died of rheumatic heart disease on 21st July, 1796, at the tragically young age of 37. When we consider that his first work was published only ten years before his death, the volume of his output is phenomenal by any standard.

Scotland's national poet, he is perhaps the only Scottish poet whom non-literary people could name with any confidence and, as such, I make no excuse for placing him at number one in this book.

TO A MOUSE

On turning her up in her nest with the plough, November 1785

Wee, sleekit, cowrin, tim'rous beastie,		*sleek / smooth-coated*
O, what a panic's in thy breastie!		
Thou need na start awa sae hasty		
Wi' bickering brattle!		*short, rapid, noisy run*
I wad be laith tae rin an' chase thee,		*loth*
Wi' murdering pattle!		*long-handled spade for cleaning plough*

5 — I wad be laith tae rin an' chase thee,

Wee, sleekit, cowrin, tim'rous beastie,   *sleek / smooth-coated*
O, what a panic's in thy breastie!
Thou need na start awa sae hasty
            Wi' bickering brattle!   *short, rapid, noisy run*
5   I wad be laith tae rin an' chase thee,   *loth*
            Wi' murdering pattle!   *long-handled spade for cleaning plough*

I'm truly sorry man's dominion
Has broken Nature's social union,
An' justifies that ill opinion
10   Which makes thee startle
At me, thy poor, earth-born companion
            An' fellow-mortal!

I doubt na, whyles, but thou may thieve;   *sometimes*
What then? poor beastie, thou maun live!   *must*
15 A daimen icker in a thrave   *odd ear;   24 sheaves*
            'S a sma request
I'll get a blessin' wi' the lave,   *what's left*
            An' never miss 't!

Thy wee-bit housie, too, in ruin!
20 Its silly wa's the win's are strewin'!   *feeble ;   winds*
An' naething, now, to big a new ane,   *build*
            O' foggage green!   *coarse grass / moss*
An' bleak December's win's ensuin',
            Baith snell an' keen!   *bitterly cold ;   piercing*

25 Thou saw the fields laid bare an' waste,
An' weary winter comin' fast,
An' cozie here, beneath the blast,
            Thou thought to dwell,
Till crash! the cruel coulter past   *iron cutter in front of ploughshare*
30   Out thro' thy cell.   *through*

That wee bit heap o' leaves an' stibble,   *stubble*
Has cost thee monie a weary nibble!
Now thou's turned out, for a' thy trouble,
            But house or hald,   *without ;   holding*
35 To thole the winter's sleety dribble   *endure*
            An' cranreuch cauld!   *hoar-frost*

But Mousie, thou art no thy lane   *not alone*
In proving foresight may be vain:
The best-laid schemes o' mice an' men
40   Gang aft agley,   *go often wrong / askew*
An' lea'e us nought but grief an' pain   *leave ;   nothing*
            For promis'd joy!

Still thou art blest, compar'd wi' me!
The present only toucheth thee:
45 But och! I backward cast my e'e,   *eye*
            On prospects drear!   *gloomy scenes*
An' forward, tho' I canna see,
            I guess an' fear!

Suggested Study Points

To a Mouse by Robert Burns

Read the poem aloud, fairly slowly.
- *No doubt there are a number of words with which you are unfamiliar:*

Check meanings given in the margin and discuss any others which remain to be clarified.

Now you are ready to study the poem more closely.

Understanding

1. **The situation**
   - What is the situation in the poem? What has happened?
   - Who is speaking in the poem, and to whom?
   - Can you suggest, in general terms, the speaker's attitude to the object of his address?

2. **The themes**
   - **At this stage in your reading of the poem**, what themes have you noticed?
     (Don't expect to get all of them at this point!)
   - Keep adding to this list as you work through the poem.

Analysis

§1: Stanzas 1–3, lines 1–18: about the mouse
   - Identify the variations in **tone**:
     e.g., in stanza 1, the poet's tone is friendly, affectionate;
   - Pick out words from each stanza, which help to identify the tone.

   - *The poet presents a vivid **image** of the mouse and its situation, helping us to picture the creature's fragility and vulnerability.*
   - Identify and note the detail provided by each word / phrase used to describe the mouse.

   - Identify and comment on the effectiveness of the **devices / techniques** used in these stanzas.

§2: Stanzas 4–6, lines 19–36: about the nest
   - Discuss:
     (a) **tone**;
     (b) further evidence towards the **image** of the mouse;
     (c) any **devices / techniques** used in these stanzas, as above.

§3: Stanzas 7–8, lines 37–48: of mice and men
   - Note how the **tone** changes at this point in the poem.
   - What causes this change of tone?

Looking over the whole poem
   - *The incident took place in the month of November, in a field, where the poet was ploughing:*
   - Pick out words / phrases from the poem which help us to picture the **setting.**

- **Poetic Form**
  The stanza form in which this poem, and many others by Burns, is written has a special name:
  - What is this form called?
  - Work out the rhyme scheme — *N.B. The rhyme needs Scottish pronunciation to work.*
  - Work out the metrical pattern.
  - Is there any connection between the two?
  - Has the poet made effective use of this poetic form?

- **Literary Form**
  - What literary form does Burns use in this poem?
    (Clue — the poet speaking to the mouse)
  - What is the effect, on the reader, of the literary form used?
  - What does it reveal of the person speaking?

- **Allegory**
  This is not just a sentimental poem about a little fieldmouse.
  Burns uses the mouse to symbolise something else about which he has very strong feelings.
  - Can you suggest what or whom the mouse symbolises? Look carefully at the poem again.
    (The clue lies in the now-proverbial lines 39–40, where the poet makes a direct comparison.)
  - Now look at the earlier stanzas to work out the allegory. Note as many examples as you can.

- **Syntax**
  You cannot have failed to notice the profusion of exclamation marks in the poem!
  - You may consider this device a little overdone, but what is their effect?

- **Language**
  Think of the language of the poem as a whole:
  - How effective and / or appropriate is it?
  - *There is a set of words, which we might call philosophical:*
    Identify and discuss the importance of those words to the meaning of the poem.
  - Why do those words stand out from the rest? To what extent do they fit into the poem?

Evaluation

- Look over your completed list of themes dealt with in the poem.
  - Some you may want to group together, as different aspects of the same theme.
  - Decide if there is one main theme or an order of priority.
  - What have you understood about the poet's attitude to the theme(s) he has presented?
  - To what extent do you agree or disagree with him? Give reasons.

- Look back on the different ways the poet has conveyed his theme(s) / attitudes to you.
  - How effectively has he done so? Are some techniques more effective than others?

- Discuss the way of life of the poor farming community depicted in the poem.

- To what extent do you consider the ideas raised in this poem to be relevant to our lives today?

- What do you understand by "Fate"?

- What was your personal response to reading the poem?
  - Comment on any aspects that you found particularly effective or appropriate.

- **Write down** one sentence summing up your final opinion of the poem.

Read the poem again quietly, to yourself, enjoy it and see how much you have gained from close study.

Using Your Notes for Revision
To a Mouse by Robert Burns

Understanding and Analysis

(Use these questions to help you revise important parts of the poem.)

1. **Look over your notes on themes:**

    (a) What theme is introduced in stanzas 1 and 2, lines 1–12?
    (b) How is this theme made clear to us?
    (c) How does the poet develop this theme in the next four stanzas, lines 13–36?
    (d) What other theme comes out of the incident with the plough?

2. **Look over your notes on tone:**

    (a) Trace the variations in tone used by the poet over the first six stanzas, lines 1–36.
    (b) For each change, note how the poet's tone is conveyed.
    (c) Note and account for the change in tone in stanzas 7 and 8, lines 37–48.
    (d) How does the language of those two stanzas help to convey the tone?

3. Note the effectiveness of the different techniques / devices used by the poet to create a vivid picture of the mouse.
    (You should have examples of lexical choice, imagery, language, poetic and literary form.)

Evaluation

(You might like to practise for the exam by writing an answer to this question.)

4. Explain, with close reference to the poem as a whole, why stanza 7, lines 37–42, is central to the main ideas in the poem, making clear the extent to which the poet has succeeded in engaging your sympathy for those ideas.   (10 marks)

    (You should deal with the allegorical nature of the poem here and make a personal response to the ideas in the poem. It might be a good idea to quote and discuss lines 39–40.)

Using Your Notes for Revision
To a Mouse by Robert Burns

Understanding and Analysis

(Use these questions to help you revise important parts of the poem.)

1. (a) What has happened at the beginning of the poem?
    (b) Who is speaking in the poem and to whom is he speaking?

2. (a) For what does the poet apologise in stanza 2, lines 7–12?
    (b) What does he say in stanzas 3–6, lines 13–36, about the problems the mouse has now?

3. **Look over your notes on the poet's presentation of the mouse:**

    How does the poet help us to understand how small and easily hurt the mouse is?
    (You should have notes on lexical choice, imagery, alliteration and onomatopoeia.)

4. **Look over your notes on tone:**

    (a) What are the poet's feelings towards the mouse?
    (b) Note the **ideas** and the kind of **language** he uses when he is talking to the mouse, which help the poet to make his feelings known.

5. Note how the poet's mood (how he is feeling) changes in stanzas 7 and 8, lines 37–48.

Evaluation

(You might like to practise for the exam by writing an answer to this question.)

6. *The poem is about more than a little mouse whose nest has been destroyed:*

    (a) What is the poem really about?   (2 marks)
    (b) Explain how the poet uses this incident to tell us about human problems, about which Burns knew only too well.   (4 marks)
    (c) Do you think this is a good way to put across his ideas?
         Try to explain how it helped you to understand what the poet meant.   (4 marks)

| **Critical Response Guide** |
| *To a Mouse* by Robert Burns |

Paragraph 1 — Introduction — include:
- title and poet's name;
- who is speaking in the poem and to whom he is speaking;
- what has happened at the beginning of the poem.

Paragraph 2:
- Write down some evidence from the poem which helped you to picture
- **where** the incident took place, and
- **at what time of year** it happened.
- Explain:
- why the mouse runs away from the poet, and
- what the poet apologises to the mouse for, in stanza 2, lines 7–12.

Paragraph 3:
- Write down some of the words which the poet uses to help us picture the mouse.
- Try to explain how each one helps us to understand how small and easily hurt the mouse is.

Paragraph 4 — How the poet feels about the mouse.
Include how he feels about:
- the mouse's stealing his corn — stanza 3, lines 13–18;
- the mouse's nest being ruined — stanzas 4 and 5, lines 19–30.
- Give some evidence from the poem to prove what you have written.

Paragraph 5: *"The best -laid schemes o' mice an' men / Gang aft agley"*
Explain:
- what the poet means by these lines;
- the poet's feelings in the last 2 stanzas, lines 37–48, and why he feels this way.

Paragraph 6: The poet uses the mouse and its situation to tell us about something else.
Explain:
- what the poem is really about , and
- how he uses the mouse's situation to illustrate human problems;
- whether you think this is a good way to put over his ideas;
- how it helped you to understand what the poet meant.

Paragraph 7 — Conclusion — include:
- whether you enjoyed reading this poem;
- anything you particularly liked / disliked / agreed with / disagreed with;
- one sentence, summing up your final impression of the poem.

WELCOME TO A BASTART WEAN

*A Poet's Welcome to his love-begotten daughter; the first instance
that entitled him to the venerable appellation of Father . . .*

Thou's welcome, wean! Mishanter fa' me,   *wee ane(one); bad luck befall me*
If ought o' thee or of thy mammy,
Shall ever daunton me or awe me,   *subdue; strike me with dread*
      My sweet, wee lady,
5   Or if I blush when thou shalt ca' me
      Tyta or Daddy!   *Dada*

What tho' they ca' me Fornicator,
An' tease my name in kintra clatter?   *country chatter*
The mair they talk, I'm kenn'd the better;   *known*
10   E'en let them clash!   *gossip*
An auld wife's tongue's a feckless matter   *feeble*
      To gie ane fash.   *to vex / annoy one*

Welcome, my bonny, sweet, wee dochter!   *daughter*
Tho' ye come here a wee unsought for,
15   And tho' your comin I hae fought for,
      Baith Kirk and Queir;   *Church and choir/ congregation*
Yet, by my faith, ye're no unwrought for . . .   *i.e., he put a lot of effort into love-making*
      That I shall swear!

Wee image o' my bonny Betty,
20   As fatherly I kiss and daut thee,   *make a pet of*
As dear and near my heart I set thee,
      Wi' as guid will,
As a' the priests had seen me get thee   *would like to have; beget*
      That's out o' H_____ .   *Hell*

25   Sweet fruit o' mony a merry dint,   *occasion of lovemaking*
My funny toil is no a' tint;   *merry, full of fun; lost, wasted*
Tho' thou cam to the warld asklent,   *irregularly (i.e. outwith marriage)*
      Which fools may scoff at;
In my last plack thy part's be in't -   *old Sco. copper coin = 1/3 of*
30   The better half o't.   *an Eng. penny of same time*

Tho' I should be the waur bestead,   *worse provided*
Thou's be as braw and bienly clad,   *finely; well, warmly*
And thy young years as nicely bred
      Wi' education,
35   As ony brat o' Wedlock's bed   *child (not really derogatory)*
      In a' thy station.   *class, social position*

Guid grant that thou may ay inherit   *God ; always*
Thy mither's looks an' gracefu' merit,
An' thy poor, worthless daddy's spirit
40   Without his failins!
'Twill please me mair to see thee heir it   *inherit*
      Than stocket mailins.   *well-stocked farms*

And if thou be what I wad hae thee,
An' tak the counsel I shall gie thee   *give*
45   I'll never rue my trouble wi' thee . . .
      The cost nor shame o't . . .
But be a loving father to thee,
      And brag the name o't.

Suggested Study Points
Welcome to a Bastart Wean by Robert Burns

Read the poem aloud, fairly slowly.

- *No doubt there are a number of words with which you are unfamiliar.*
  Check meanings given in the margin and discuss any others, which remain to be clarified.

Now you are ready to study the poem more closely.

Understanding

1. **The situation**
   - What is the situation in the poem?
   - Who is speaking in the poem, and to whom?
   - Can you suggest, in general terms, the speaker's attitude to the object of his address?

2. **The themes**
   - At this stage in your reading of the poem, what themes have you noticed?
     (Don't expect to get all of them at this point!)
   - Keep adding to this list as you work through the poem.

Analysis

§1: *Stanza 1, lines 1–6, sets the **tone** of **tenderness** for the child — "wean", line 1, "My sweet wee lady", line 4;*
   - and of **delight at the child's birth** — *the wholehearted welcome to the child in the first words of the poem — "Thou's welcome, wean!" — runs through the whole poem.*
   - Note these examples and amass further evidence of this tone as you work through the remaining stanzas.

§2: *Stanza 2, lines 7–12, introduces the poet's critics:* Who are they?
   - Identify and account for the poet's **attitude** to those people.
   - How is this attitude made clear to you?
   - Identify and comment on the effectiveness of the **device** in line 11: "an auld wife's tongue".

§3: *In **stanzas 3 and 4**, lines 13–24, we see the poet's **attitude** to the Kirk and ministers:*
   - Identify his attitude and explain how it is made clear to you.
   - Identify and comment on the effectiveness of the **device** in line 16: "Baith Kirk and Queir".

§4: *In **stanzas 4 and 5**, lines 19–30, we see the poet's **attitude** to the child's mother and to their lovemaking:*
   - Identify and comment on his attitude. How is it made clear to you?
   - Identify and comment on the effectiveness of the **metaphors** in lines 25, 26 and 27.
   - Who are the "fools" referred to in line 28? What is his reason for calling them fools?

§5: *In **stanzas 6 to 8**, lines 31–48, the poet expresses his hopes for the child's future:*
   - What does the poet promise and hope for his daughter in the future?
   - Identify and comment on the effectiveness of the **device** in line 35 "Wedlock's bed".
   - What **attitude** does he display towards the child's mother in lines 37–38?
   - What **tone** comes into lines 39–40? What do those lines reveal of the poet's character?
   - What is the **tone** of the final lines of the poem? How does he build up to the last line?

Looking over the whole poem

- Discuss the **title** and the **subtitle**: *One was the poet's choice, the other his publisher's.*
- Can you identify which is which? Give reasons for your choice.

- **Poetic Form**:
- What name is given to the stanza form in which this poem is written?
- Work out the rhyme scheme — *N.B. The rhyme needs Scottish pronunciation to work.*
- Work out the metrical pattern. Is there any connection between the two (rhyme and metre)?
- Has the poet made effective use of this poetic form?

- What **literary form** does Burns use in this poem?
- What is the effect, on the reader, of the literary form used?
- What does it reveal of the person speaking?

- How effective / appropriate is the **language** of the poem as a whole?

- **Contrast:** Look again at the first two stanzas:
- *Stanza 1 — the poet welcomes his child, says he will never be ashamed or embarrassed by her;*
- *Stanza 2 — deals with the gossips who malign him because of the child's birth;*
- *the **juxtaposition** of these two stanzas introduces the contrast that goes through the whole poem.*
- What two things are being contrasted?
- Look for particular words in these two stanzas which emphasise the contrast.
- *Sometimes the juxtaposition is within stanzas.*
- Examine the rest of the poem and note examples of juxtaposition which sustain the contrast.
- *The **poetic form** is used to point up this contrast.* If you missed this aspect when discussing the poet's effective use of the poetic form, look now at stanza 5, lines 25–30, which is a good example.

- What two things are being contrasted in stanza 6, lines 31–36? How is the contrast achieved?
- What two things are being contrasted in stanza 7, lines 37–42? How is the contrast achieved?

Evaluation

- Look over your completed list of themes dealt with in the poem.
- Some you may want to group together, as different aspects of the same theme.
- Decide if there is one main theme or an order of priority.
- What have you understood about the poet's attitude to the theme(s) he has presented?
- To what extent do you agree or disagree with him? Give reasons.

- Look back on the different ways the poet has conveyed his theme(s) / attitudes to you.
- How effectively has he done so? Are some techniques more effective than others?

- What was your personal response to reading the poem?
- Comment on any aspects that you found particularly effective or appropriate.
- From your reading of this poem, what is your impression of the poet?

- **Write down** one sentence summing up your final opinion of the poem.

Read the poem again quietly, to yourself, enjoy it and see how much you have gained from close study.

Using Your Notes for Revision
Welcome to a Bastart Wean by Robert Burns

Understanding and Analysis

(Use these questions to help you revise important parts of the poem.)

1. **Look over your notes on the themes.**

   (a) What theme is introduced in stanza 1?
   (b) How does the poet develop this theme?
   (c) What theme is introduced in stanza 2, lines 7–12?
   (d) Note the poet's development of this theme.

2. **Look over your notes on tone.**

   (a) Note the changes in tone in the course of the poem.
   (b) For each change, note how the poet achieves that tone.

3. **Look over your notes on contrast.**
   (a) Note your ideas on the contrast between the two titles.
   (b) Note the various ideas and techniques / devices which carry on that contrast very effectively throughout the poem.
   (As well as ideas, you should have covered lexical choice, juxtaposition and poetic form.)

Evaluation

(You might like to practise for the exam by writing an answer to this question.)

4. *(a)* What impression of the poet do you have from your reading of this poem?   **(7 marks)**

   (b) To what extent do you think he is justified in the attitudes he reveals?   **(3 marks)**

   (You should try to see the poet's weaknesses as well as his good qualities, and, in judging his enemies, take into account the times in which they lived.)

Using Your Notes for Revision
Welcome to a Bastart Wean by Robert Burns

The poet shows his delight at the birth of his first child, a girl born to Betty Paton, his mother's servant girl, on 22nd November, 1785; he and the child's mother were not married.

Understanding and Analysis

(Use these questions to help you revise important parts of the poem.)

1. (a) To whom is the poet speaking in the poem?
    (b) What does the poet say to this person in the first stanza, lines 1–6?
    (c) What does he promise her, in stanza 6, lines 31–36?
    (d) What hopes for her future does he express in stanza 7, lines 37–42?

2. **Look over your notes on the poet's attitudes.**

    (a) How does the poet **feel** about the child?
    (b) Check that you can find evidence to support your answer at *(a)*.

    The poet expresses strong feelings against some other people in the poem.
    (c) Who are those people?
    (d) What feelings towards them does he express?
    (e) Find some evidence from the poem to support your answer at *(d)*.

3. **You are told in the introductory note that this poem was written in 1785.**
    (a) Without that note, how could you tell from the poem itself that it was not written in modern times?
    (b) Pick out some evidence from the poem to support your answer.

Evaluation

(You might like to practise for the exam by writing answers to these questions.)

4. From your reading of the poem, what kind of person do you think the poet is? Give reasons to back up your opinions.   (5 marks)
    (You should consider the poet's weaknesses as well as his good qualities.)

5. (a) Did you enjoy reading this poem?
        What did you like and / or dislike in the poem?   (3 marks)

    (b) Try to give reasons for the things you liked or disliked about the poem.   (2 marks)

Critical Response Guide

Welcome to a Bastart Wean by Robert Burns

In this poem, the poet is delighted to welcome his first child, a daughter born to Betty Paton, a servant girl of his mother's, on 22nd November, 1785. The poet did not marry the child's mother and he was strongly criticised by the Church and the community.

Paragraph 1 — Introduction — include:

- title and poet's name;
- who is speaking in the poem and to whom he is speaking;
- what the poet says to this person in the first stanza.

Paragraph 2 — Include:

- how the poet **feels** about the child;
- evidence to support your statement about his feelings for the child;

- what he promises the child, in stanza 6, lines 31–36 + evidence;

- his hopes for her future, expressed in stanza 7, lines 37–42 + quotations.

Paragraph 3 — *The poet expresses strong feelings against some other people in the poem.* **Include:**

- who these people are, and

- his feelings towards them + quotations.

Paragraph 4 — Include:

- (From your reading of this poem) your impression of poet;
- reasons / evidence from the poem to back up your opinions.

Paragraph 5 — Conclusion — include:

- whether you enjoyed reading this poem;

- what you liked and / or disliked in the poem;
- reasons for your likes / dislikes;

- one sentence summing up your final impression of the poem.

HOLY WILLIE'S PRAYER
And set the godly in a pet to pray. (Pope)

Background to the poem
Holy Willie (William Fisher) was a middle-aged bachelor, an Elder in the parish of Mauchline (Ayrshire). Willie and his minister, Mr. Auld had just lost a case, brought by them before the Presbytery of Ayr, against Gavin Hamilton, who was accused of setting out on a journey on a Sunday, and of making one of his servants dig potatoes from the garden on another Sunday. Willie and Auld were humiliated in the process. The poet imagines overhearing Willie at prayer:

1.

O Thou, wha in the Heavens dost dwell
Wha, as it pleases best Thysel,
Sends ane to Heaven and ten to Hell,
    A' for Thy glory,
5   And no for ony guid or ill
      They've done afore Thee.

2.

I bless and praise Thy matchless might,
Whan thousands Thou hast left in night,
That I am here, afore Thy sight,
10   For gifts and grace,
A burnin' and a shinin' light
    To a' this place.

3.

What was I or my generation,   *family*
That I should get sic exaltation?   *such*
15 I, wha deserve sic just damnation
    For broken laws,
Five thousand years 'fore my creation,
    Through Adam's cause.

4.

When frae my mither's womb I fell,
20 Thou might hae plunged me into Hell
To gnash my gums, to weep and wail,
    In burnin' lake,
Whare damnéd devils roar and yell,
    Chain'd to a stake.

5.

25 Yet I am here a chosen sample,
To show Thy grace is great and ample;
I'm here a pillar in Thy temple,
    Strong as a rock,
A guide, a buckler, an example,   *ruler*
30   To a' Thy flock.

6.

O Lord, Thou kens what zeal I bear
When drinkers drink, and swearers swear
And singing there, and dancing here,
    Wi' great and sma';
35 For I am keepit by Thy fear,   *kept; fear of you*
    Free frae them a'.   *from*

(The poem is continued on pages 24 and 25.)

Suggested Study Points
Holy Willie's Prayer by Robert Burns

The poem has been split to make it easier for you to work with.

Read the whole poem aloud, fairly slowly.
- *No doubt there are a number of words with which you are unfamiliar.*
- Check meanings given in the margin and discuss any others which remain to be clarified.

Now you are ready to study the poem more closely.

Understanding

1. **The situation**
   - What is the situation in the poem?
   - Who is speaking in the poem, and to whom?
   - What is the purpose of the prayer?

2. **The themes**
   - **At this stage in your reading of the poem**, what themes have you noticed? *(Don't expect to get all of them at this point!)*
   - Keep adding to this list as you work through the poem.

Analysis

§1: Stanzas 1–6
- **Register:** *The register of the poem is set in stanza 1, starting with the first line of the poem:*
- What kind of language is this? Note other examples from this section.
- ** Add to your list as you read through the poem.

- **Tone:** *also established in the first stanza: long vowel sounds in "Thou", "Wha", "A";*
- *give a lofty, resounding tone, appropriate to an exceedingly pious person at prayer.*
- Look for more examples of that tone in the first 5 stanzas.
- ** Add to your list as you read on.

- Pick out words which reveal the **absurdity of Willie's beliefs**.
- Discuss the effectiveness of each word or set of words — how they achieve their aim.

- Discuss the vivid **image** of Hell presented in stanza 4.
- Note any other **linguistic or literary devices / techniques**, discussing, for each example, the effectiveness of the device / technique and what it contributes to the poem.

- **Contrast:** *Throughout the poem there is an **ironic** contrast between the prayer form and what Willie is actually saying to God.*
- What do you expect to find in the words and sentiments of a prayer?
- To what extent does Willie's prayer fulfil your expectations?
- Give examples of areas which appear inappropriate to a prayer.
- What is the **effect** of this discrepancy?   ** Add further examples as you read.

- Discuss the linking function of stanza 6.

7.

But yet, O Lord! confess I must,
At times I'm fash'd wi fleshly lust;   *troubled*
And sometimes, too, wi' warldly trust,
40   Vile self gets in;
But Thou remembers we are dust,
        Defil'd in sin.

8.

O Lord! yestreen, Thou kens, wi' Meg —   *knows*
Thy pardon I sincerely beg,
45 Oh, may't ne'er be a livin' plague,
        To my dishonour,
And I'll ne'er lift a lawless leg
        Again upon her.

9.

Besides, I farther maun avow,   *must declare*
50 Wi' Lizzie's lass, three times I trow —   *believe*
But, Lord, that Friday I was fou   *drunk*
        When I came near her,
Or else, Thou kens, Thy servant true
        Wad ne'er hae steer'd her.   *molested*

10.

55 Maybe Thou lets this fleshly thorn
Beset Thy servant e'en and morn,
Lest he owre high and proud should turn,   *too*
        'Cause he's sae gifted;
If sae, Thy han' maun e'en be borne
60   Until Thou lift it

11.

Lord, bless Thy chosen in this place,
For here Thou hast a chosen race;
But God confound their stubborn face,
        And blast their name,
65 Wha bring Thy elders to disgrace
        And public shame.

12.

Lord, mind Gawn Hamilton's deserts,
He drinks, and swears, and plays at cartes,   *cards*
Yet has sae mony takin' arts,   *is so charming*
70   Wi' great and sma'
Frae God's ain priests the people's hearts
        He steals awa.

13.

And when we chasten'd him therefore,
Thou kens how he bred sic a splore,
75 And set the world in a roar
        O' laughin' at us; —
Curse Thou his basket and his store,
        Kail and potatoes.   *cabbage*

14.

Lord, hear my earnest cry and prayer
80   Against the presbyt'ry of Ayr;
Thy strong right hand, Lord, mak it bare
                Upo' their heads,
Lord, weigh it down, and dinna spare,
                For their misdeeds.

15.

85   O Lord, my God, that glib-tongued Aiken,
My very heart and saul are quakin',
To think how we stood groanin', shakin',
                And swat wi' dread,   *sweated*
While he, wi' hingin' lip and snakin',   *sneering*
90   Held up his head.

16.

Lord, in the day of vengeance try him
Lord, visit them wha did employ him,
And pass not in Thy mercy by 'em,
                Nor hear their prayer;
95   But for Thy people's sake destroy 'em,
                And dinna spare.

17.

But, Lord, remember me and mine,
Wi' mercies temp'ral and divine,
That I for gear and grace may shine,   *wealth*
100   Excell'd by nane,
And a' the glory shall be Thine,
                Amen, Amen!

§2: Stanzas 7–10
- • Pick out and discuss words which reveal **Willie's hypocrisy** in this section.
- • Discuss the effectiveness of the **metaphor** in line 45.
- - Discuss the effectiveness of any other linguistic **devices / techniques** in this section.
- ** **Add to your list** of examples of **register**, variations in **tone** and evidence of **contrast**.

§3: Stanzas 11–16
- • Find further evidence of **Willie's hypocrisy** in this section.
- - Pick out and discuss words which reveal his **vicious spite**.
- ** **Add to your list** of examples of **register**, variations in **tone**, evidence of **contrast**, and discuss the effectiveness of any linguistic or literary **devices / techniques** in this section.

§4: Stanza 17
- • Pick out and discuss words which reveal his **material greed.**
- • Find further evidence of the **contrast** between prayer form and content.
- ** Discuss variations in **tone** and further evidence of **Willie's hypocrisy** in this stanza.

Looking over the whole poem

- **Structure:** *The poem divides naturally into four sections.*
- Identify the sections and state briefly what each section deals with.
- **Satire:** *(See definition in **Some Useful Definitions** at the end of this book.)*
- Who or what is / are the target(s) of this satire?
  - What kind of God does Willie reveal to us in the first four stanzas?
  - How does the poet make Willie appear ridiculous in our eyes?
  - How does the poet's treatment of Willie contribute to the satire?
- Consider how the **juxtaposition** of the sections contributes to the satire.

- **Literary Form:**
- What elements of a prayer can you detect in the poem?
- What literary form does Burns use in this poem?
  - The speaker is not the poet; what is the literary term used to denote such a speaker?
  - Can you suggest why the poet chose to write as someone other than himself in this poem?
- What does the speaker reveal about himself?

- **Poetic Form:**
  - *The stanza form in which this poem, and many others by Burns, is written has a special name.*
  - What is it?
  - Work out the **rhyme scheme** — *N.B. The rhyme needs Scottish pronunciation to work.*
  - Work out the **metrical pattern**. Is there any connection between the two (rhyme and metre)?
- Has the poet made effective use of this poetic form?

Evaluation

- Look over your completed list of the **themes** dealt with in the poem.
  - Some you may want to group together, as different aspects of the same theme.
  - Decide if there is one main theme or an order of priority.

- What have you understood about the **poet's attitude** to the theme(s) he has presented?
  - To what extent do you agree or disagree with him? Give reasons.
  - Do the themes you have been discussing hold any **relevance** to modern day life?

- Look back on the different ways the poet has conveyed his theme(s) / attitudes to you.
  - How effectively has he done so? Are some techniques more effective than others?

- What was your **personal response** to reading the poem?
  - Comment on any aspects that you found particularly effective or appropriate.

- **Write down** one sentence summing up your final opinion of the poem.

Read the poem again quietly, to yourself, enjoy it and see how much you have gained from close study.

Using Your Notes for Revision
Holy Willie's Prayer by Robert Burns

Understanding and Analysis

(Use these questions to help you revise important parts of the poem.)

1. **Look over your notes on the Calvinist religion and make sure you understand:**

    (a) the Doctrine of Predestination;
    (b) Original Sin;
    (c) the Calvinists' picture of Hell / damnation;
    (d) the Calvinists' idea of what God is like.

2. **Make sure you understand the definition of Satire on page 163.**

    (a) What was the poet's purpose in writing this poem?
    (b) How does he use
       (i)   poetic and literary form and
       (ii) structure
       to achieve his purpose?

3. **Revise your notes on** the effectiveness of the linguistic and literary **techniques / devices** used by the poet to convey his satire.
    (You should have covered lexical choice, contrast, imagery, and any others you have noticed in the poem.)

Evaluation

(You might like to practise for the exam by writing an answer to this question.)

4. *(a)* How does your impression of the persona differ from his own idea of himself?

    (6 marks)

    (b) To what extent do you agree with the poet's attitude to the persona and to the ideas expressed in the poem?

    (4 marks)

    (You should discuss, in detail, and comment on any particular features of Willie and of his beliefs of which you strongly approve or disapprove.)

Using Your Notes for Revision

Holy Willie's Prayer by Robert Burns

In this poem, the poet imagines that he overhears Willie praying.

Understanding and Analysis

(Use these questions to help you revise important parts of the poem.)

1. What does Willie tell us about his God in stanzas 1 to 3, lines 1–18?

2. What does Willie say to God in stanzas 7 to 10, lines 37–60?

3. What is Willie's main reason for praying to God (stanzas 11–16)?

4. **Look over your notes on the description of Hell in stanza 4:**
   (a) How does the poet help us to imagine Willie's idea of Hell?
   (b) How does this picture fit in with the kind of God you discussed in your answer to question 1?

5. **Look over your notes on stanzas 11–16:**
   (a) What strong feelings does Willie express in those stanzas?
   (b) Note some evidence from the poem to support your answer.

6. **Look over your notes on Literary Form:**
   (a) In what ways is this poem like a prayer?
   (b) Note the ways in which it is not like a prayer.

Evaluation

(You might like to practise for the exam by writing answers to these questions.)

7. What is your impression of Willie? What kind of man is he?   (4 marks)

8. (a) How do you think the poet feels about Willie and his religion?
   (The title of the poem may give you a clue.)   (3 marks)

   (b) Do you agree or disagree with the poet?
   Give reasons for your answer.   (3 marks)

Critical Response Guide
Holy Willie's Prayer by Robert Burns

In this poem, the poet imagines that he overhears Willie praying.

Paragraph 1 — Introduction — include:
- title and poet's name;
- who is speaking and to whom he is speaking.

Paragraph 2 — Include:
- what Willie tells us about God in **stanza 1**, lines 1–6;
- what Willie confesses to God in **stanzas 7 to 10**, lines 37–60;
- what Willie asks God to do in **stanzas 11 to 16,** lines 61–96.

Paragraph 3 — Include:
- the place which the poet describes in **stanza 4,** lines 19–24;
- how he helps us to imagine this place — quote and explain;
- how this picture fits in with the kind of God you discussed in para. 2.

Paragraph 4 — In stanzas 11 to 16, lines 61–96, Willie expresses strong feelings against some people. Explain:
- who these people are;
- why Willie feels this way about them.
- Describe the feelings Willie expresses in those stanzas.
- Write down some evidence from the poem to show how strongly he feels.

Paragraph 5 — Include:
- what you would expect a prayer to be like;
- the ways in which this poem is **like** a prayer;
- the ways in which it is **not like** a prayer.

Paragraph 6 — Include:
- your impression / opinion of Willie;
- how you think the poet feels about Willie and his religion;
  (The title of the poem may give you a clue.)
- whether you agree or disagree with the poet + reasons.

Paragraph 7 — Conclusion — include:
- whether you enjoyed reading the poem;
- anything you particularly enjoyed / admired / agreed with / disagreed with;
- one sentence giving your final impression of the poem.

SUCH A PARCEL OF ROGUES IN A NATION

In 1695, the entire wealth of Scotland was invested in a plan to establish a colony on the isthmus of Panama, with a view to operating a trading company from this base. By 1698, the plan, called the Darien Scheme, had failed, many lives were lost and Scotland was bankrupt.

In 1707, 52 years before Burns was born, members of the Scottish Parliament were allegedly bribed to vote for union with the English Parliament. The Union must have been seen as a life-saver by the Scottish government, with no resources to run the country, but many Scots, including Burns, regarded these MSPs as rogues and traitors.

1.

Fareweel to a' our Scottish fame,
  Fareweel our ancient glory;
Fareweel ev'n to the Scottish name,   *It was fashionable to call Scotland*
  Sae fam'd in martial story!   *North Britain*
5   Now Sark rins over Solway sands,   *river at west end of Sco/Eng border*
  And Tweed rins to the ocean,   *river at east end of Sco/Eng border*
To mark where England's province stands —
  Such a parcel of rogues in a nation!

2.

What force or guile could not subdue
10   Thro' many warlike ages,
Is wrought now by a coward few
  For hireling traitors' wages.
The English steel we could disdain
  Secure in valour's station;
15   But English gold has been our bane —
  Such a parcel of rogues in a nation!

3.

O would, or I had seen the day   *I wish; before / rather than*
  That Treason thus could sell us,
My auld grey head had lien in clay   *lain*
20   Wi' Bruce and loyal Wallace!
But pith and power, till my last hour   *without/ though I no longer have*
  I'll mak this declaration:—   *pith and power*
"We're bought and sold for English gold" —
  Such a parcel of rogues in a nation!

Unseen Textual Analysis
Such a Parcel of Rogues in a Nation by Robert Burns

All answers should be supported by close reference to the text.

1. *(a)* Show how the syntax of lines 1–4 has helped you to understand the
           speaker's mood and why he feels this way.   (2) AU
    (b) Comment on the poet's use of contrast in this stanza.   (1) A
    (c) Comment on the tone of "England's province", line 7, and explain the
           importance of this phrase in the context of the poem.   (2) AU

2. *(a)* Explain the additional idea that is introduced in line 8.   (1) U
    (b) How is that idea developed in stanza 2?   (2) U
    (c) Comment on the effectiveness of 2 examples of lexical choice in
           lines 9–12, which reinforce the idea introduced in line 8.   (4) A

3.   *"English steel"*, line 13; *"English gold"*, line 15.
    (a) Explain how these 2 phrases encapsulate the speaker's argument.   (2) U
    (b) By referring closely to the rest of the poem, show how effectively the poet
           uses military / monetary metaphors to reinforce his argument.   (4) A

4. *(a)* How does the stance of the persona change in the last stanza?   (2) A
    (b) Identify and account for the change of tone in lines 21–23.   (2) A

5. *(a)* How effective do you find the poet's use of a persona?   (4) E
    (b) To what extent has the speaker engaged your sympathy   (4) E
           for his cause?
    (Before answering (b), it might help to read over the paragraph printed above the
    poem.)

Total Marks (30)

> # Unseen Textual Analysis
> ## *Such a Parcel of Rogues in a Nation* by Robert Burns

The following information is given above the poem:

1. *Between 1695 and 1698, Scotland's money was lost in a business venture, leaving the country bankrupt.*
2. *Nine years later, the Scottish Parliament joined up with the English Parliament.*
3. *A few Scots were allegedly bribed to vote for the Union.*
4. *These people were called "traitors" by many of their countrymen.*

Keep these points in your mind as you answer the following questions.

1. *The first 3 lines of the poem begin with the word "Fareweel".*
Explain, in your own words as far as possible, to whom or what the speaker is saying goodbye. (1) U

2. *(a)* According to the speaker in lines 5–7, what has happened? (2) U
(b) Write down the phrase from stanza 1 which refers to Scotland. (1) U

3. *(a)* Who are the rogues referred to in the title? (1) U
(b) What did those people do? (2) U
(c) Write down **one** phrase from lines 9–12 which helps you to understand what those people did. (1) A
(d) How does the speaker feel about those "rogues"? (2) A
(e) Write down a **different** phrase from lines 9 -12 which tells you how the speaker feels about those people. (1) A

4. *(a)* What is meant by "English steel" in line 13? (2) U
(b) What does the speaker say about "English steel" in lines 13–14? (2) U
(c) Write down another phrase from the same stanza which **contrasts** with "English steel". (1) A
(d) Explain why the poet makes this contrast. (2) U

5. *(a)* What physical details do we find out about the speaker from stanza 3? (2) U
(b) What is the tone of his words in lines 17–20? (1) A
(c) What is the tone of his words in lines 21–22? (1) A
(d) Write down some evidence from this stanza to support each of your answers at *(b)* and *(c)*. (2) A

6. *(a)* How do you feel about the speaker in the poem? (1) E
(b) Referring to the poem, explain why you feel this way. (3) E
(c) Has the speaker convinced you that Scotland was betrayed by some members of the Scottish Parliament or can you suggest a good reason for their actions? Remember to justify your answer. (2) E

Total Marks (30)

Suggestions for Critical Essays

(For general guidance on writing critical essays, see page 165.)

1. Select one poem dealing with the world of nature — plants / animals — and, by close examination of the poet's techniques / devices, show to what extent he is commenting, not merely on the world of nature, but on some aspect of human emotion or behaviour.

    [This question is suitable for *To a Mouse*. **Use your discussion notes**.]

2. Explain what you believe to be the essential "message" contained in any poem you know well. Show how the skill of the poet, in constructing the poem and in choosing words and language features, has given power to the message and contributed to your enjoyment of the poem.

    [This question is suitable for any of the poems in this chapter. **Use your discussion notes**.]

3. A dramatic monologue can reveal a character clearly, merely by the words he / she speaks. By close examination of the poetic techniques / devices used, show the skill with which the poet does this in a monologue you have read, and discuss how the poet's attitude is also revealed.

    [This question is suitable for *Holy Willie's Prayer*. **Use your discussion notes**.]

4. Choose a poem in which satire is used to ridicule the Establishment of the day. By referring to one poem, show how effective you consider this device to be in putting across the poet's personal feelings and / or beliefs.

    [This question is suitable for *Holy Willie's Prayer*. **Use your discussion notes**.]

5. Compare and contrast two poems by the same writer and, by close reference to the techniques / devices used in both poems, explain which, in your opinion, has put across the stronger message.

    [This question is suitable for *Welcome to a Bastart Wean* and *Holy Willie's Prayer*. **Use your discussion notes for both poems**.]

Some Ideas and Suggestions for Writing

(For general guidance on writing essays for Language Study Unit, see page 168.)

1. **"Scotland is a country of recurrent depression, betrayal, surrender, grim-faced intolerance."**
    Prepare a debating speech, either supporting or opposing this motion.
    (This is expressive writing: a **persuasive** essay; or creative writing: a **dramatic speech**.)

    It will be necessary to know the way a debate is organised and to remember that this is a speech, which should be obvious from the language used and from frequent interjections of phrases like "ladies and gentlemen", "friends", fellow-students", etc. You may regard this as the first speech, in which case no reference will be made to the opposition, or as the second speech, in which case you may refer to points made in your opponent's speech, in order to demolish them. Consider the historical reasons behind the wording of the motion. Make sure you have a strong concluding sentence. If you choose the dramatic option, you may use a persona.

2. **Write, in a humorous tone, about your ideas of Heaven or Hell or both.**
    (This is creative writing: a piece of **prose fiction** or a **dramatic script** or a **poem**.)

    You may like to write in stream of consciousness style, as if you have just arrived in your personal Heaven or Hell, or simply reflect on what would constitute Heaven or Hell, or both, for you.

3. **Write an essay on any type of fanaticism or obsession or hypocrisy about which you feel strongly.**
    (This is expressive writing: a **persuasive** essay; or creative writing: a **dramatic monologue / speech**.)

    Although the subject of this essay is something about which you feel strongly, this is not a piece of personal writing. Your feelings will often be implicit in your reasoned discussion. Beware of sounding as fanatical as the people you are criticising! Make sure that you are well informed on the topic you are discussing; don't work on the "everybody knows what those . . . are like" principle. This kind of essay lends itself to a good deal of irony. If you choose the dramatic option, you may use a persona.

4. **Love makes the world go round. Love is blind. Love's a banana skin . . .**
    Write about love in any way you like.
    (This is expressive writing: a **personal reflective** essay; or creative writing: a **poem** or set of poems.)

    It's probably best not to give away any of your secrets! You may treat the subject seriously or humorously. You may want to write about the love you have witnessed of a parent for a disabled child, your grandparents' love for each other after a long marriage . . . or perhaps about a spotty boy's / girl's love for the school heart throb / hunk, your own unsuccessful encounters with a member of the opposite sex — the ridiculous (now) ways you engineered meetings only to remain unnoticed . . . the possibilities are endless. If you choose the poetry option, consider two or three poems depicting different kinds of love in the same person, e.g., a woman's love for child / husband / father . . .

CHAPTER 2
Hugh MacDiarmid:

The Watergaw and *Lo! a Child is Born*

HUGH MACDIARMID, 1892–1978

The poet and his work

After Burns, the next poetic giant and trendsetter to emerge in Scotland was Christopher Murray Grieve, alias Hugh MacDiarmid. He was born and brought up in Langholm in the Scottish Borders, near which small town a beautiful monument, bearing some of the symbols associated with the poet's work, now adorns a bare moor. This geographical location was a lifelong influence on his writing. His experience was predominantly rural, as is the imagery he uses; as a rule, cities feature in his poetry as places to avoid. He was an intelligent observer of the Scottish character, which he saw as being composed of opposing attributes, a condition grandly titled "The Caledonian Antisyzygy" by Gregory Smith in his *Scottish Literature, Character and Influence*. Many of his poems rely for their impact largely on the same juxtaposition of opposites.

The poet was brought up in a home where books and religion were the staple diet. His father was the Librarian in Langholm and the young Christopher would go upstairs to the library with a laundry basket and fill it with books to take down to his room. As a young man, he was a keen student of the Bible but declared himself an atheist in later life. Despite this declaration, his work contains and often centres on Christian ideas, but they are generally used ironically.

Grieve fought in World War I and, on his return home from the War, he continued to fight, this time for the revival of the Scots language as a vehicle for complex intellectual ideas rather than what he regarded as the sentimental slush which had been produced by the so-called Kailyard school of literature. He abhorred and rebelled against the Lallans of the self-styled "makars" and the Scottish fiction writers of the late 19th / early 20th centuries. MacDiarmid, of course, had to go to the other extreme!

> *"I'll hae nae hauf-way hoose, but aye be whaur*
> *Extremes meet . . ."*   (From *A Drunk Man Looks at the Thistle*)

He was trying to effect nothing less than a Scottish Literary Renaissance but came up against considerable opposition. Feeling that colloquial Scots had been degraded by the Kailyard writers, he searched dictionaries to find obsolete words, which had the merit of being fresh, for his first Scots poems. He said poetry was "not an idea gradually shaping itself in words but deriving entirely from words . . . it was in this way that I wrote all the best of my Scots poems". The first of these poems, and one of the loveliest, is the first poem in this chapter.

A founding member of the SNP, he was thrown out of that organisation for being a Communist, only to be expelled from the Communist Party for being a Nationalist! In truth, it's hard to put a label on him. He was an iconoclast with a mischievous sense of humour, never happier than when he was stirring things up. In *A Drunk Man*, he slates the one-day-a-year Burns lovers, thus:

> *"No' wan in fifty kens a wurd Burns wrote . . .*
> *. . . Mair nonsense has been uttered in his name*
> *Than ony's barrin' liberty and Christ."*

Friend and fellow poet Norman MacCaig observed that MacDiarmid's death should have been marked by a "two-minute pandemonium".

Like Burns, MacDiarmid is translated, read and admired all over the world.

THE WATERGAW

Ae weet forenicht i' the yow-trummle
I saw yon antrin thing,
A watergaw wi' its chitterin' licht
Ayont the on-ding;
5   An' I thocht o' the last wild look ye gied
Afore ye deed!

There was nae reek i' the laverock's hoose
That nicht — an' nane i' mine;
But I hae thocht o' that foolish licht
10   Ever sin' syne;
An' I think that mebbe at last I ken
What your look meant then.

ae weet forenicht: one wet afternoon / early evening
yow-trummle: literally, sheep-tremble: cold weather after sheep-shearing
antrin: rare
watergaw: indistinct / watery rainbow
chitterin' licht: shivering light
ayont the on-ding: after the onset / heavily falling rain
thocht: thought; gied: gave
deed: died
reek: smoke ; laverock's: lark's (proverbial phrase: it was cold and stormy)
sin' syne: since then

Suggested Study Points
The Watergaw by Hugh MacDiarmid

Read the poem aloud, fairly slowly.

- *No doubt there are a number of words with which you are unfamiliar.*
  Check meanings given in the glossary and discuss any others which remain to be clarified.

Now you are ready to study the poem more closely.

Understanding

1. **The situation**
    - Who is speaking in the poem, and to whom?
    - State **briefly** what the speaker says in the poem.

2. **The themes**
    - **At this stage in your reading of the poem**, what themes have you noticed? *(Don't expect to get all of them at this point!)*
    - Keep adding to this list as you work through the poem.

Analysis

§1: Stanza 1, lines 1–6
- What can you deduce from the first stanza about the **setting**?

- How would you describe the **tone** in lines 1–4?
- How is this tone made clear to you?

- What **mood** is created in the first line of the poem and by what means?
- How appropriate is this mood to the subject of the poem?

- Identify words / phrases which create an **image** of cold and dreariness in the first stanza.
- Discuss the effectiveness of each image.

- How does the **tone** change in lines 5–6?

- The poem starts as narrative; at which point do you realise that it is more than that?

§2: Stanza 2, lines 7–12
- What further change in **tone** do you notice in lines 7–8?
- Discuss the effectiveness of the **device** used in those lines, which helps to create this further change of tone.
- Consider the appropriateness to the theme of this **cold imagery**, begun in stanza 1.

- Identify words and phrases which link the poet's father's death to the elements / Nature.
- Discuss the effectiveness of this cosmic **imagery**.

- What is meant by "that foolish licht" in line 9?
- Consider all of the implications of "foolish".

- What is the **tone** in lines 11–12?
- Do you detect an undercurrent to this tone? (Think of "foolish", line 9.)

- Comment on the way the poem ends.

Looking over the whole poem
- *An **extended comparison** runs throughout the poem:*
- Which two things are compared?
- Discuss the effectiveness of the different words / phrases / devices which contribute to this comparison.
- Consider the **irony** of the comparison, in the light of the ideas presented in the poem.

- What kind of **language** is used in the poem?
- Identify and discuss individual words which you consider to be particularly effective.
- Work out what makes these words effective.

Poetic Form
- Look at the way the poem is laid out : is it regular or irregular?
- Work out the rhyme scheme.
- Work out the metrical pattern.
- Is there any connection between the two?
- Has the poet made effective use of this poetic form?

Literary Form
- What literary form does MacDiarmid use in this poem?
- What is the effect, on the reader, of the literary form used?
- What does it reveal of the person speaking?

Evaluation

- Look over your completed list of themes dealt with in the poem.
- Some you may want to group together, as different aspects of the same theme.
- Decide if there is one main theme, or an order of priority.
- What have you understood about the poet's attitude to the theme(s) he has presented?
- To what extent do you agree or disagree with him? Give reasons.

- Look back on the different ways the poet has conveyed his theme(s) / attitudes to you.
- How effectively has he done so? Are some techniques more effective than others?

- To what extent does the title indicate the sense of the poem?
- How does MacDiarmid move from the particular to the universal in this poem?

- What was your personal response to reading the poem?
- Comment on any aspects that you found particularly effective or appropriate.

- **Write down** one sentence summing up your final opinion of the poem.

Read the poem again quietly, to yourself, enjoy it and see how much you have gained from close study.

Using Your Notes for Revision
The Watergaw by Hugh MacDiarmid

Understanding and Analysis

(Use these questions to help you revise important parts of the poem.)

1. **Make sure you understand the kind of language MacDiarmid uses in this poem:**
    (a) Note the meanings of the more interesting words in the poem.
    (b) What do those words add to the poem?

2. **Summarise the situation** dealt with in the poem and note the extent to which the title conveys the sense of the poem.

3. **Look over your notes on tone:**
    Identify and account for each change in tone throughout the poem.

4. **Look over your notes on Poetic and Literary Form:**
    Note how the poetic and literary forms used have contributed to your understanding of the poet's mood.

5. **Revise your notes on the effectiveness of the devices / techniques** used to create a vivid picture of the scene at the poet's father's death-bed.
    (You should have covered the extended cold imagery; extended comparison of the rainbow and the man's dying look; and the poet's use of puns to reinforce the comparison.)

6. **Make sure you understand the poet's use of irony**.

Evaluation

(You might like to practise for the exam by writing an answer to this question.)

7. Explain how MacDiarmid moves from the particular to the universal in this poem, making clear the extent to which you find yourself approving of the attitudes he reveals.
    (10 marks)

    (Try to see the poet's thought processes: watergaw → look in father's eyes → mystery of death.)

Using Your Notes for Revision
The Watergaw by Hugh MacDiarmid

Understanding and Analysis

(Use these questions to help you revise important parts of the poem.)

1. **Make sure you understand the kind of language MacDiarmid uses in this poem:**
   - *(a)* Note the meanings of the more interesting words in the poem.
   - *(b)* What do those words add to the poem?

2. *(a)* Who is speaking in the poem and to whom?
   - *(b)* Explain briefly what he is saying.

3. **Think about the title** of the poem.
   - *(a)* What is the importance of the watergaw in the poem?
   - *(b)* The poem is not really about the watergaw though; explain what the real subject of the poem is.

4. **Look over your notes on setting**:
   - *(a)* Note words / phrases which tell you that the poem is set in the country.
   - *(b)* Explain, if necessary, how each word makes you aware of the setting.

5. **Pick out and explain some words / phrases** which refer to weather:
   - *(a)* when the poet saw the watergaw;
   - *(b)* on the night of his father's death.
   - *(c)* How does the poet's description of the weather help us to understand how he felt when his father died?

Evaluation

(You might like to practise for the exam by writing an answer to these questions.)

6.   *"An' I think that mebbe at last I ken*
             What your look meant then."   lines 11–12

   - *(a)* What is it that the poet thinks he now knows?   (2 marks)
   - *(b)* How sure is he?   (1 mark)
   - *(c)* Quote from the poem to support your last answer.   (1 mark)

7. What is your response to the poet in this poem?   (6 marks)

(Do you feel sorry for the poet at any point in the poem? Explain why / why not. Is there any point in the poem where your feelings were different from those stated in your last answer? Explain why / why not.)

Critical Response Guide
The Watergaw by Hugh MacDiarmid

Paragraph 1 — Introduction — include:
- title and poet's name;
- who is speaking in the poem and to whom he is speaking;
- what the poet says to this person in the first stanza.

Paragraph 2 — include:
- where the poem is set — city or country + evidence.

Paragraph 3 — Explain:
- what the weather was like when the poet saw the watergaw,
- quote / explain / comment on evidence to support your statement;
- what the weather was like on the night his father died,
- quote / explain / comment on evidence to support your statement.

Paragraph 4 — include:
- how you think the poet felt when his father died,
- quote / explain / comment on evidence to support your statement.

Paragraph 5 — include:
- what the poet thinks he now knows;
- how sure he is + quote / explain / comment;
- your impression of the kind of man the poet is, based on this poem.

Paragraph 6 — include:
- whether you feel sorry for the poet at any point in the poem + reasons;
- whether your feelings changed at any point in the poem + reasons.

Paragraph 7 — Conclusion — include:
- whether you enjoyed reading the poem, and
- what you particularly liked and / or disliked about the poem + reasons;
- one sentence summing up your final impression of the poem.

LO! A CHILD IS BORN

I thought of a house where the stones seemed suddenly changed
And became instinct with hope, hope as solid as themselves,
And the atmosphere warm with that lovely heat,
The warmth of tenderness and longing souls, the smiling anxiety
That rules a home where a child is about to be born.
The walls were full of ears. All voices were lowered.
Only the mother had the right to groan or complain.
Then I thought of the whole world. Who cares for its travail
And seeks to encompass it in like lovingkindness and peace?
There is a monstrous din of the sterile who contribute nothing
To the great end in view, and the future fumbles,
A bad birth, not like the child in that gracious home
Heard in the quietness turning in its mother's womb,
A strategic mind already, seeking the best way
To present himself to life, and at last, resolved,
Springing into history quivering like a fish,
Dropping into the world like a ripe fruit in due time —
But where is the Past to which Time, smiling through her tears
At her new-born son, can turn crying: "I love you"?

> ## Suggested Study Points
> *Lo! a Child is Born* by Hugh MacDiarmid

Read the poem aloud fairly slowly.

Understanding

1. **The situation**
    - Who is speaking in the poem, and to whom?
    - Summarise, **briefly**, what he is talking about.

2. **The themes**
    - **At this stage in your reading of the poem**, what themes have you noticed?
      (Don't expect to get all of them at this point!)
    - Keep adding to this list as you work through the poem.

Analysis

Structure
   - Identify the natural divisions in the poem, justifying your decisions.

§1: lines 1–7
   - What tone is indicated in the first line of the poem?
   - How is that **tone** developed in the rest of this section?

   - Identify and discuss the effectiveness of the devices / techniques used, in lines 1–7, to create a vivid **image** of the household awaiting the birth of a child.
   - How does the **syntax** of this section add to that image?

§2: lines 8–12
   - Identify the **tone** created in the first line of this section.
   - How is this tone made clear to you?

   - Identify and discuss the effectiveness of the devices / techniques used in this second section to present a **comparison / contrast** with the previous section.

   - How does the **tone** change in line 10?

§3: lines 12–17
   - How is the **contrast** introduced in this section?
   - Discuss the effectiveness of the devices used in this section to continue the **comparison / contrast** with the previous section.

   - Identify and discuss the effectiveness of the two **similes** in this section.
   - *In each case consider:*
     (a)   what is being compared to what;
     (b)   what the points of comparison are;
     (c)   what is achieved by making the comparison.

   - Explain the **irony** of these similes, in the light of the poet's argument.

§4: lines 18–19

- *The **comparison / contrast** continues*; how is it introduced in this section?
- Identify and discuss any words / phrases linking back to previous sections.

- What **tone** do you detect in the final lines of the poem?
- How is it made clear to you?

- Identify and discuss the effectiveness of the **devices / techniques** used in the final section of the poem.

- Consider the effectiveness of this section as a fitting **conclusion** to the poem.
- What is the effect of the final question mark?

Looking over the whole poem

- Identify and discuss the effectiveness of the Christian **imagery / allusions** used throughout the poem.
- Explain the **irony** of the poet's use of Christian imagery / allusions to put across his ideas.

- **Poetic Form:**
- Look at the way the poem is laid out: is it regular or irregular?
- Is there any rhyme and / or metrical pattern?
- Has the poet made effective use of this poetic form?

- **Literary Form:**
- What literary form does MacDiarmid use in this poem? *(Clue — one person speaking.)*
- What is the effect, on the reader, of the literary form used?

Evaluation

- Look over your completed list of themes dealt with in the poem.
- Some you may want to group together as different aspects of the same theme.
- Decide if there is one main theme or an order of priority.

- What have you understood about the poet's attitude to the theme(s) he has presented?

- To what extent do you agree or disagree with him? Give reasons.
- Consider the possibility of the opposing sides in his argument being compatible.

- Look back on the different ways the poet has conveyed his theme(s) / attitudes to you.
- How effectively has he done so? Are some techniques more effective than others?

- To what extent does the title indicate the sense of the poem?

- What was your personal response to reading the poem?
- Comment on any aspects that you found particularly effective or appropriate.

- **Write down** one sentence summing up your final opinion of the poem.

Read the poem again quietly, to yourself, enjoy it and see how much you have gained from close study.

Using Your Notes for Revision
Lo! A Child is Born by Hugh MacDiarmid

Understanding and Analysis

(Use these questions to help you revise important parts of the poem.)

1.   Summarise the **situation** in the poem and outline the **argument** put forward by the poet.

2.   Note the **structure** of the poem and the linking words which signal each change of view.

3.   **Look over your notes on tone**:
     Note textual references which show how the tone varies in accordance with the **structure** of the poem.

4.   **Revise your notes on the effectiveness of the devices / techniques** used to underline the contrast between the two sides of the poet's argument.
     (You should have notes on imagery, alliteration, personification, repetition, lexical choice, oxymoron, cliché, caesura, juxtaposition and anthropomorphism.)

Evaluation

(You might like to practise for the exam by writing an answer to this question.)

5.   *(a)*   How successful do you think MacDiarmid is in his use of Christian
             imagery to put across his humanist beliefs?   (7 marks)

             *(You will want to deal with the poet's use of irony; think about the
             connotations of the title.)*

     (b)   To what extent does this imagery help you to understand the poet's
             message?   (3 marks)

Using Your Notes for Revision
Lo! A Child is Born by Hugh MacDiarmid

Understanding and Analysis

(Use these questions to help you revise important parts of the poem.)

1. *(a)* Who is speaking in the poem?
    (b) Explain briefly what he is saying.

2. *The poem divides clearly into four (unequal) sections.*
    For each section:
    (a) note the line numbers and first and last words;
    (b) explain, in more detail, what each section is about;
    (c) explain **how the poet feels** about what he is saying, giving some evidence.

3. **Look over your notes on lines 1–7, imagery:**
    Note, and make sure you understand, some of the words / phrases, which create an atmosphere of warmth and love in the house where the child is about to be born.

4. **Look over your notes on lines 8–12, comparison / contrast:**
    (a) What are these lines about?
    (b) Make sure you understand the image in lines 8–12 *(middle of the line)*: to what does he compare the world?
    (c) Pick out and explain some words / phrases which emphasise the **contrast** between the births of the human child and of the world.

5. *"Springing into history, quivering like a fish"* — line 16
    "Dropping into the world like a ripe fruit in due time," — line 17

    (a) What is the poet talking about in the lines quoted above?
    (b) Revise your notes on the effectiveness of these **similes**.

Evaluation

(You might like to practise for the exam by writing an answer to this question.)

6. *(a)* From your study of this poem, what have you understood about the
        poet's religious beliefs?   (4 marks)
        (You should refer to the poem in your answer.)

    (b) Write about one or more parts of the poem, which you particularly like
        and which have helped you to understand the poet's ideas.   (6 marks)

    *(Consider, for example, the way the poet writes about the world as if it were the
    child of Time or God, or write about any of the images or similes . . . perhaps the
    poem reminded you of the birth of a baby in your family.)*

Critical Response Guide
Lo! a Child is Born by Hugh MacDiarmid

Paragraph 1 — Introduction — include:
- title and poet's name;
- who is speaking in the poem;
- what he is saying.

Paragraph 2: Work through each of the four (unequal) sections. For each one:
- write down the line number and first and last words;
- explain, in more detail, what each section is about.

Paragraph 3: For each section:
- explain how the poet feels about what he is saying;
- give some evidence for each feeling you have identified.

Paragraph 4: Pick out and explain:
- some words / phrases, which create an atmosphere of warmth and love in the house where the child is about to be born;
- some words / phrases which emphasise the **contrast** between the births of the human child and of the world.

Paragraph 5: Explain:
- what you have understood from this poem about the poet's religious beliefs;
- whether you agree or disagree with the poet, giving reasons.

Paragraph 6 — Conclusion — include:
- whether you enjoyed reading the poem;
- any parts of the poem which you particularly enjoyed or disliked, saying what you liked or disliked about these parts;
- one sentence summing up your final impression of the poem.

WITH THE HERRING FISHERS

"I see herrin'." — I hear the glad cry
And 'gainst the moon see ilka blue jowl
In turn as the fishermen haul on the nets
And sing: "Come shove in your heids and growl."

5   "Soom on, bonnie herrin', soom on," they shout
Or "Come in, O come in, and see me."
"Come gie the auld man something to dae.
It'll be a braw change frae the sea."

O it's ane o' the bonniest sichts in the warld
10   To watch the herrin' come walkin' on board
In the wee sma' 'oors o' a simmer's mornin'
As if o' their ain accord.

For this is the way that God sees life,
The haill jing-bang o's appearin'
15   Up owre frae the edge o' naethingness
— It's his happy cries I'm hearin'.

"Left, right — O come in and see me,"
Reid and yellow and black and white
Toddlin' up into Heaven thegither
20   At peep o' day frae the endless night.

"I see herrin'," I hear his glad cry,
And 'gainst the moon see his muckle blue jowl
As he handles buoy-tow and bush-raip
Singin': "Come shove in your heids and growl!"

Unseen Textual Analysis
With the Herring Fishers by Hugh MacDiarmid

All answers should be supported by close reference to the text.

1. *(a)* Drawing your information from stanzas 1 and 2, show how the poet conveys the impression that the herring fishers are fairly "rough and ready" men. (2) U

   (b) In those same lines, how does he convey a quite different impression of those men? (2) U

2. *"For this is the way that God sees life"*, line 13.

   (a) Show the importance of this line to the structure of the poem, making clear how the words link back to the first three stanzas. (2) A

   (b) Explain the relationship between the two parts of the poem. (2) A

   (c) Demonstrate, with detailed reference to the text, how the poet uses repetition or echoing words / phrases to make this relationship clear. (4) A

3. *(a)* Comment on the effectiveness of the image in stanza 3 (lines 9 – 12) of the herring being brought on board in the nets. (2) A

   (b) Explain, briefly, how he offsets this picture against another image later in the poem. (1) A

   (c) Referring closely to the two extended images, explain what this technique contributes to the impact of the whole poem. (5) A

4. This is "a poem of two halves" (to paraphrase the football reporters' cliché). In which "half" do you think you detect the genuine voice of the poet? (10) E
   (Refer closely to the poem to justify your decision.)

Total Marks (30)

Unseen Textual Analysis
With the Herring Fishers by Hugh MacDiarmid

---

1. Look closely at stanzas 1 and 2, lines 1–8.
    What is your impression of the herring fishers from those lines?
    (You should consider and give some examples from those stanzas of:
    (a) their appearance;
    (b) how they talk;
    (c) the kind of job they do;
    (d) how they feel about their work.)   (4) UA

2. *The poem divides neatly into two halves.*

    Explain, **in your own words**,
    (a) what stanzas 1 to 3, lines 1–12, are about,   (2) U
    (b) what stanzas 4 to 6, lines 13–24, are about.   (2) U
    (c) Explain how the two halves are connected to each other.   (2) A
    (d) Give **two** examples from each half which show this connection.   (2) A

3. *(a)* In stanza 3, lines 9–12, how does the poet describe the herring?   (2) A
    (b) Which **one** of the following words best conveys what you think of
        this description?
             frightening   funny   realistic   sinister   (1) E
    (c) Give a reason for your answer at *(b)*.   (2) E

4. *(a)* In stanzas 4 and 5, lines 13–20 what is the poet describing?   (2) A
    (b) What do you think of this description?   (1) E
    (c) Give a reason for your answer at *(b)*.   (2) E

5. *Think about this question: Why do fishermen catch fish?*

    (a) With your answer to the question in mind, what might the poet be
        saying about God, when he compares Him to the fishermen?   (3) E
    (b) What do you think the poet's attitude to God is?   (2) E

6. Write a paragraph explaining what you like and / or dislike about the
    poem, giving reasons for your opinions.   (3) E

Total Marks (30)

Suggestions for Critical Essays

(For general guidance on writing critical essays, see page 165.)

1.   Poetry is often written as a result of an intense emotional experience.
Examine the techniques used by one poet to convey the significance of an experience which gave rise to a poem.

[This question is suitable for *The Watergaw*. **Use your discussion notes**.]

2.   Choose a poem which was initially difficult for you because of such things as its subject, language, theme, word choice . . .
Briefly outline the difficulty and in greater detail explain in what ways closer study of the poet's techniques made the experience of reading it worthwhile.

[This question is suitable for *The Watergaw*. **Use your discussion notes**.]

3.   Choose a poem in which the poet uses an everyday event to convey his own strongly-held ideas and show how the devices and techniques which he uses have helped you to understand his ideas.

[This question is suitable for *The Watergaw* and *Lo! a Child is Born*. **Use your discussion notes**.]

4.   It is often thought that poetry is solely about serious and sad subjects. Select a poem which is about a happy event, a joyful experience, a fulfilling emotion . . . Closely examine the techniques / devices which make you both enjoy and understand what is being communicated to you.

[This question is suitable for *Lo! a Child is Born*. **Use your discussion notes**.]

5.   Compare and contrast two poems by the same writer which deal with the same or similar themes and, by close reference to the techniques / devices used in each poem, explain which one, in your opinion, has put across the message more strongly.

[This question is suitable for the two poems discussed in this chapter; it could also be used to compare one of those with the unseen poem, *With the Herring Fishers*, if that poem has also been discussed in detail. **Use your discussion notes**.]

Some Ideas and Suggestions for Writing

(For general guidance on writing essays for Language Study Unit, see page 168.)

1. **MacDiarmid enjoyed being controversial, especially with regard to established ideas and beliefs. Which area of the establishment makes you angry enough to want to abolish / destroy it?**
    (This is expressive writing: a **persuasive** essay; or creative writing: a **dramatic monologue / speech**.)
    You might consider such areas as The House of Lords, the monarchy, any law which you consider to be repressive, unjust . . . or you may interpret the word "establishment" very loosely, to cover areas closer to your experience like young people's rights, school rules, police harassment, the internet . . . You may treat the subject in a humorous / lighthearted way, as long as it makes a serious point.

2. **Have you ever been profoundly affected by some aspect of Nature?**
    (This is expressive writing: a **personal reflective** essay; or creative writing: a **poem** or set of poems.)
    The possibilities here are endless . . . perhaps you have seen a foal / calf / lamb being born; come across a wild animal in its own habitat; been moved by a beautiful dawn or sunset, exhilarated by a fierce thunder storm . . . Start by describing, in detail, the aspect of Nature which stirred your emotions. Describe and try to account for the feelings evoked in you by this incident / event. Explain in what way, if any, you were changed by it. This would be a good topic for poetry-writing; e.g., two poems: Sunrise . . . Sunset)

3. **Write about the occasion of a birth or a death in your family.**
    (This is expressive writing: a **personal reflective** essay.)
    State the occasion you are writing about.
    You may describe the event but the greater part of your essay should deal with the feelings within the family and your reflections on the significance of the occasion.

4. **Write a short story, in which the main character(s) is / are engaged in a stressful job or profession, in the course of which a job-related crisis occurs.**
    (This is creative writing: a piece of **prose fiction**.)
    *You may think of particularly dangerous occupations like firemen, soldiers; lonely ones like night-watchmen; useful ones like doctors, nurses, social workers; glamorous ones like footballers, pop stars, film stars; stressful ones like the last category whose every move is catalogued by the media . . . **BUT** don't forget this is a story: something has to happen . . .*

5. **Write a short story or a dramatic script, in which the main character seeks help from a supernatural source.**
    (This is creative writing: a piece of **prose fiction** or a **dramatic script**.)
    The "supernatural source" may involve prayer, consulting a fortune teller, a Ouija board . . . Think about the problem facing your character. Does he / she seek help from earthly sources — if not, why not; if yes, why not successful? What are his / her feelings leading up to his / her approach to the supernatural source? Is the problem resolved? If so, in what way? Whichever form you choose, you might like to start with the approach to the supernatural source and reveal the problem in the course of the consultation . . . do it as a flashback rather than a narration, in order to inject some drama into your writing. Be careful with the lead in and out of flashback.

CHAPTER 3

Edwin Muir:

Childhood and *The Horses*

EDWIN MUIR, 1887–1959

The poet and his work

Edwin Muir, a contemporary of MacDiarmid's, was born at Deerness on the tiny island of Wyre in the Orkneys. His island childhood is powerfully evoked in the first poem of this chapter, *Childhood*, and the kind of farming community, in which he grew up, is the foundation of the second poem, *The Horses*. It is not surprising then to find such precise detail in his poems, especially in his description of working horses, which were part of his early life. (See plate at the front of this book.)

He moved to Glasgow with his family when he was 14 years old and this change of scene was traumatic for Muir. For the first time, he saw people living in poverty and squalor of a kind which did not exist among the island community, however poor. He walked through the Gorbals every day to his job as a clerk and writes of the experience in his autobiography thus: "These journeys filled me with a sense of degradation . . . the arrogant women, the mean men, the terrible children . . ." His view may have been coloured by the deaths of both parents and his two elder brothers within five years of coming to the city. He married Willa Anderson in 1919 and moved to London where he worked as a journalist for a left-wing literary and political journal. Not surprisingly, considering the losses he had suffered, he was by this time in a highly neurotic state. He underwent psychoanalysis, which led to vivid dreams and waking visions, on which much of his early poetry is based.

He had been brought up in a small community, whose traditions and ritual had not changed over the last century; he called this pattern of the past The Fable, and saw each individual's life as a re-enactment of that pattern, which he called The Story. He is very much concerned with the past and how it affects the present. In *An Autobiography*, he writes: ". . . we receive much more than we can ever give; we receive it from the past, on which we draw with every breath, but also . . . from the Source of the mystery itself, by the means of which religious people call Grace."

Although he did become more interested in Christian dogma during his time in Europe, particularly in Rome, he was not a member of a church but he was very conscious of the mystery of life, an awareness that permeates his poetry. He believed childhood to be an idyllic state, a sort of Eden, an intuitive state lost to adults; similarly in society he saw the past as pure, wholesome, but as society has "grown up", we have fallen from grace, lost that innocence and sensitivity to the mystery of life, destroyed by our developing knowledge and technological advances. It is easy to imagine his feelings, were he alive today, about current scientific discoveries like cloning.

The language of his poetry is English with an archaic feel which comes from the different syntax and speech rhythms of his native Orkney, influenced as it has been by its Norse history. He admired MacDiarmid's work but disagreed with his attempts to revive the Scots language, believing that Scotland could only "create a national literature by writing in English", as a result of which the irascible MacDiarmid conducted a prolonged campaign against him.

Muir returned from Europe in 1950 and, with his wife, took up the post of Warden of Newbattle Abbey, an adult education college, where he taught for the next five years. One of his students was fellow-Orcadian George Mackay Brown, the poet featured in the next chapter.

CHILDHOOD

Long time he lay upon the sunny hill,
      To his father's house below securely bound.
Far off the silent, changing sound was still,
      With the black islands lying thick around.

5   He saw each separate height, each vaguer hue,
      Where the massed islands rolled in mist away,
And though all ran together in his view
      He knew that unseen straits between them lay.

Often he wondered what new shores were there.
10   In thought he saw the still light on the sand,
The shallow water clear in tranquil air,
      And walked through it in joy from strand to strand.

Over the sound a ship so slow would pass
      That in the black hill's gloom it seemed to lie.
15   The evening sound was smooth like sunken glass,
      And time seemed finished ere the ship passed by.

Grey tiny rocks slept round him where he lay,
      Moveless as they, more still as evening came,
The grasses threw straight shadows far away,
20   And from his house his mother called his name.

Suggested Study Points
Childhood by Edwin Muir

Read the poem aloud fairly slowly.

Understanding

1. **The situation**
    - Summarise, **briefly**, what the poem is about.
    - Look for opposing impressions - e.g. positive / negative, good / bad.

2. **The themes**
    - **At this stage in your reading of the poem**, what themes have you noticed?
      (Don't expect to get all of them at this point!)
    - Keep adding to this list as you work through the poem.

Analysis

Stanza 1, lines 1–4:
- *A strong sense of place is created in this poem*. Note references to the **setting**.

- What **mood** is created in stanza 1? How is this atmosphere made clear to you?
- Pay particular attention to contrasting words in line 3: what is their effect?
- How does this mood fit in with the theme(s)?

- Discuss the **sound effects** in stanza 1. *(Look for echoes of those effects through the poem.)*
- What contribution do those effects make to the general theme(s) of the poem?

- Identify and discuss the effectiveness of **images** created by the poet in the first stanza, to convey the child's feeling of security.

Stanza 2, lines 5–8:
- Note references to the **setting**. What is the effect of the **repetition** in line 5?
- How does the poet create a sense of unity in the landscape?
- Note contrasting words which create a sense of balance and harmony in the landscape.

- How does the **mood** change as the boy's view stretches to include landscape further off?
- How does line 8 introduce a contrary sense of what awaits the child in the future?
- Which word in line 7 indicates the approach of the contrary view?
- How does this change of mood contribute to the theme(s)?

Stanza 3, lines 9–12:
- What does the boy imagine the outside world to be like? Why does he picture it thus?
- What is the effect of this innocent dream on the reader?
- How does the poet create the dream-like **atmosphere** in stanza 3?
- Discuss the slightly different **sound effect** created in this stanza.

Stanza 4, lines 13–16:
- Note references to the **setting** — what is the effect of the ship's appearance in the bay?

- How is the **mood**, created by the ship's appearance, continued in line 14?
- How does this mood change in the second half of the stanza?
- Pay particular attention to the **simile** in line 15 and the effect of **pun** on the word "sound".

Stanza 5, lines 17–20:
- Note references to the **setting**.
- How does the poet use the setting to help create a feeling of security for the child?

- Discuss the **mood** of stanza 5 and how it is created.

- Discuss the effect of mentioning the boy's father in line 2 and his mother in the last line.
- What is the effect of the repetition in line 20?

Looking over the whole poem:
- Discuss:
  - (a) the contribution made by the **landscape** to the atmosphere of the poem;
  - (b) how the **mood** created is fundamental to the ideas expressed by the poet;
  - (c) the connection between the boy and the landscape.
- Can you suggest why the poet goes into so much detail in his description of the landscape?

- Look at the pattern of **mood** over the five stanzas:
- What is the effect of this mixing of moods?
- How does this pattern contribute to the overall impact of the poem?
- Can you account for the mixed feelings permeating the poem?

Poetic Form
- Look at the way the poem is laid out: is it regular or irregular?
- Is there any rhyme and / or metrical pattern?
- If so, note and account for any variations from the pattern.

- Has the poet made effective use of this poetic form?

Literary Form
- What literary form does Muir use in this poem?
- What features of this form do you recognise?
- Does it help to put across the poet's ideas?

Evaluation

- Look over your completed list of themes dealt with in the poem.
- Some you may want to group together, as different aspects of the same theme.
- Decide if there is one main theme or an order of priority.

- What have you understood about the view of childhood presented in the poem?
- To what extent do you agree or disagree with this view? Give reasons.

- Look back on the different ways the poet has conveyed his theme(s) / attitudes to you.
- How effectively has he done so? Are some techniques more effective than others?

- What was your personal response to reading the poem?
- Comment on any aspects that you found particularly effective or appropriate.

- **Write down** one sentence summing up your final opinion of the poem.

Read the poem again quietly, to yourself, enjoy it and see how much you have gained from the close study.

Using Your Notes for Revision
Childhood by Edwin Muir

Understanding and Analysis

(Use these questions to help you revise important parts of the poem.)

1. Summarise the **situation** presented in the poem.

2. **Look over your notes on setting** in the poem:
   How does the setting contribute to the poet's presentation of his ideas about childhood?

3. **Look over your notes on mood / atmosphere** and revise:
   (a) how the poet creates mood / atmosphere;
   (b) the effectiveness of the devices / techniques used by the poet to create a particular mood / atmosphere;
   (You should have notes on metaphor, imagery, lexical choice, pun, sound effects, pathetic fallacy, personification and contrast.)
   (c) how that mood / atmosphere contributes to the overall impact of the poem.

Evaluation

(You might like to practise for the exam by writing an answer to this question.)

4. Referring closely to the poem, consider the effectiveness of Muir's portrayal of childhood, making clear the extent to which you agree with him. (10 marks)

   (Think about the picture he presents of childhood — peaceful, secure, innocent — and how he conveys this picture. Remember that the poem is written by an adult, who has been very unhappy, looking back. In your personal response, be careful not to stray too far from the ideas in the poem.)

Using Your Notes for Revision
Childhood by Edwin Muir

Understanding and Analysis

(Use these questions to help you revise important parts of the poem.)

1. What is the poem about?

2. What does the boy in the poem imagine the outside world will be like?

3. What is the poet saying about childhood?

4. **Look over your notes on setting.**
   (a) Pick out some details of the boy's surroundings.
   (b) What kind of place is it?
   (c) Why do you think the poet goes into so much detail about the boy's surroundings?

5. **Look over your notes on mood / atmosphere.**
   (a) How do you think the boy feels about this place?
   (b) How does the poet bring in the idea of the grown-up world outside the little island where the boy lives?
   (c) What feelings does the poet give us about the outside world?
   (d) How do these feelings fit in with what he is saying about childhood?

Evaluation

(You might like to practise for the exam by writing answers to these questions.)

6. *(a)* When you were reading this poem, did you feel the little boy had a happy life or an unhappy life?
   (b) Try to explain why you felt this way.   (5 marks)

7. Do you think the poet has given us a realistic picture of childhood in this poem? Give a reason for your opinion.   (5 marks)

Critical Response Guide
Childhood by Edwin Muir

Paragraph 1 — Introduction — include:

- title and poet's name;
- a brief explanation of what the poem is about;
- what the poet is saying about **childhood**.

Paragraph 2 — Include:

- a description of the kind of **place** where the boy is;
- some details from the poem about the boy's surroundings;

- why you think the poet goes into so much detail about this place;
- how you think the boy **feels** about this place.

Paragraph 3 — Include:

- how the poet brings in the idea of the **grown-up world outside** the little island where the boy lives;

- the impression which the poet give us about the outside world — better than the boy's home area or not?
- Some evidence from the poem which gives you this impression;

- what the poet is saying about the adult world outside the boy's home area.

Paragraph 4 — Include:

- your impression of the **kind of life** the boy in the poem has — happy or unhappy?
- Try to explain why you think he is happy / unhappy.

Paragraph 5 — Include:

- whether you think the poet has given us a **realistic** picture of childhood in this poem;
- a reason / reasons for your opinion.

Paragraph 6 — Conclusion — include:

- whether you **enjoyed** reading the poem;
- the things you most enjoyed;
- any particular feature of the poem which helped you to understand the poet's ideas;
- one sentence summing up your final impression of the poem.

THE HORSES

Barely a twelvemonth after
The seven days war that put the world to sleep,
Late in the evening the strange horses came.
By then we had made our covenant with silence,
5   But in the first few days it was so still
We listened to our breathing and were afraid.
On the second day
The radios failed; we turned the knobs; no answer.
On the third day a warship passed us, heading north,
10 Dead bodies piled on the deck. On the sixth day
A plane plunged over us into the sea. Thereafter
Nothing. The radios dumb;
And still they stand in corners of our kitchens,
And stand, perhaps, turned on, in a million rooms
15 All over the world. But now if they should speak,
If on a sudden they should speak again,
If on the stroke of noon a voice should speak,
We would not listen, we would not let it bring
That old bad world that swallowed its children quick
20 At one great gulp. We would not have it again.
Sometimes we think of the nations lying asleep,
Curled blindly in impenetrable sorrow,
And then the thought confounds us with its strangeness.
The tractors lie about our fields; at evening
25 They look like dank sea-monsters couched and waiting.
We leave them where they are and let them rust:
'They'll moulder away and be like other loam'.
We make our oxen drag our rusty ploughs,
Long laid aside. We have gone back
30 Far past our fathers' land.
                                    And then, that evening
Late in the summer the strange horses came.
We heard a distant tapping on the road,
A deepening drumming; it stopped, went on again
35 And at the corner changed to hollow thunder.
We saw the heads
Like a wild wave charging and were afraid.
We had sold our horses in our fathers' time
To buy new tractors. Now they were strange to us
40 As fabulous steeds set on an ancient shield
Or illustrations in a book of knights.
We did not dare go near them. Yet they waited,
Stubborn and shy, as if they had been sent
By an old command to find our whereabouts
45 And that long-lost archaic companionship.
In the first moment we had never a thought
That they were creatures to be owned and used.
Among them were some half-a-dozen colts
Dropped in some wilderness of the broken world,
50 Yet new as if they had come from their own Eden.
Since then they have pulled our ploughs and borne our loads,
But that free servitude still can pierce our hearts.
Our life is changed; their coming our beginning.

Suggested Study Points
The Horses by Edwin Muir

Understanding

1. **The situation**
   - What has happened?
   - What are the negative aspects of this event? Are there any positive aspects?

2. **The themes**
   - **At this stage in your reading of the poem**, what themes have you noticed?
     (Don't expect to get all of them at this point!)
   - Keep adding to this list as you work through the poem.

Analysis

Structure:

> *This poem is not broken up into neat stanzas. It is, however, possible to break it into workable sections for the purposes of analysis.*

- Look at the poem again and work out what those sections might be. Justify your division.

§1: lines 1–4
- *The **register** is set in the first few lines.*
- What is it? Find evidence to support your statement.
- How would you describe the overall literary form?
- What features of this form can you detect in the poem?
- What is the function of this first section?

- Consider the significance of the "seven days war": What **analogy** is being drawn here?
- Comment on the effectiveness of any **devices / techniques** in this section, which help you to understand what has happened and the poet's attitude to the event.

§2: lines 5–30
   (a) **lines 5–12:**
- How do those lines continue the **analogy**?
- What **mood / atmosphere** is created in lines 5–6?
- Look at the **line layout** and **syntax** of the whole section. How do they support the mood?
- How does the **tone** of the section help to create the mood?

- What do the warship and plane represent?
- Comment on the use of the word "dumb" in line 12.

   (b) **lines 12–15:**
- What **image** is presented in lines 12–15? Comment on the effectiveness of this image.
- Comment on any other devices / techniques in this section.

   (c) **lines 15–20:**
- What **tone** is apparent in lines 15–20? Find evidence to support your statement.
- Discuss the effects of the **repetition** in this section.
- Comment on the **image** created in lines 19–20.
- How does the punctuation add to the impact of the image?

(d) **lines 20−23:**
  - How does the **tone** change in lines 20−23?
  - Comment on the effectiveness of the **image** presented in those lines.

(e) **lines 24−30:**
  - Comment on the effectiveness of the **imagery** in lines 24−30.
  - What is the effect of the **direct speech** in line 27?

§3: lines 31–50

(a) **lines 31–32:**
  - What is the **function** of lines 31−32 in terms of structure?
  - What is suggested by the **juxtaposition** of those lines with lines 28−30?

(b) **lines 33–37:**
  - What **effect** is created in lines 33−35? How is it created?
  - Comment on the effectiveness of the **image** presented in lines 36−37.

(c) **lines 38–50:**
  - Comment on the effectiveness of the **imagery** in lines 40−41.
  - How do those images tie in with the overall register of the poem?

  - What is meant by the **phrase** "that long-lost archaic companionship", line 45?
  - How do the lines before and after that line (lines 42−47) lead up to and develop that phrase?

  - What **tone** do you detect in lines 48−50?
  - Consider the significance of those lines to the meaning of the whole poem.

§4: lines 51 − 53
  - How do those lines fit into the structure of the poem?
  - Comment on the **phrase** "free servitude", line 52.
  - How effective is **line 53** as a concluding line?

Poetic Form:
  - Discuss the poetic form used here.
  - Has the poet made effective use of this form?

Evaluation

  - Look over your completed list of themes dealt with in the poem.
  - Some you may want to group together, as different aspects of the same theme.
  - Decide if there is one main theme or an order of priority.
  - Look back on the different ways the poet has conveyed his theme(s) / attitudes to you.
  - How effectively has he done so? Are some techniques more effective than others?

  - To what extent is the poem a product of the times in which it was written?
  - In what way(s), if any, is the poem relevant to our lives today?
  - Do you consider the poem to be optimistic or pessimistic?
  - What was your personal response to reading the poem?
  - Comment on any aspects that you found particularly effective or appropriate.

  - **Write down** one sentence summing up your final opinion of the poem.

Read the poem again quietly, to yourself, enjoy it and see how much you have gained from close study.

Using Your Notes for Revision
The Horses by Edwin Muir

Understanding and Analysis

(Use these questions to help you revise important parts of the poem.)

1. Summarise the **situation** presented in the poem and explain the significance of the horses referred to in the title.

2. **Look over your notes on tone:**
    Trace and account for the variations in tone in the course of the poem.

3. **Look over your notes which deal with the evil of nuclear war:**
    Revise the effectiveness of the **devices / techniques** used by the poet to convey this evil.
    (You should have notes on euphemism, irony, litotes, Biblical analogy, line layout, syntax, imagery, pun, repetition and simile.)

Evaluation

(You might like to practise for the exam by writing an answer to this question.)

4. To what extent would you agree that, although it deals with the aftermath of the destruction of civilisation as we know it, this is not a depressing, pessimistic poem?   (10 marks)

    (You may, of course, disagree with the statement in the question but do not disagree on the grounds of the evil of nuclear war, as this is not what the poem is really about. Think of Muir's attitude and you will be on the right lines.)

Using Your Notes for Revision
The Horses by Edwin Muir

Understanding and Analysis

(Use these questions to help you revise important parts of the poem.)

1. What happened **before the horses came**?

2. How did people react to the horses **when they first arrived**?

3. How has the arrival of the horses **changed the people** in the poem?

4. **Read over lines 5–12 carefully.**
   (a) Pick out some details of what happened before the horses came.
   (b) How long did it take for the survivors to lose all traces of other life?
   (c) Why did the poet choose this number of days?

5. **Look again at lines 12–20.**
   (a) How does the poet help us to understand what the silence was like?
   (b) How would the survivors behave if the radios should start to work again?
   (c) Why would they behave that way?

6.   *"That old bad world that swallowed its children quick*
            At one great gulp."
   (a) What is the poet describing in those lines?
   (b) Explain why this is a good description.

7. (a) To what does the poet compare the tractors lying unused in the fields?
   (b) Why is this a good comparison?

8. How does the poet help us to imagine the sound of the horses coming nearer and nearer?

Evaluation

(You might like to practise for the exam by writing an answer to this question.)

9. **The poem tells the story of civilisation having been destroyed by nuclear attack.** Although it deals with a disaster on a huge scale, do you think the poem has a happy or a sad ending? Give reasons for your answer.   (10 marks)

   (Think of the way the poet describes the horses and what he might be saying about our present society. Muir believed that we need to get back in touch with Nature.)

Critical Response Guide
The Horses by Edwin Muir

Paragraph 1 — Introduction — include:

- title and poet's name;
- a brief explanation of what the poem is about:
- what happened **before the horses came**.
- how people reacted to the horses **when they first arrived**;
- how the arrival of the horses has **changed the people** in the poem.

Paragraph 2 — Include:

- some details, from lines 5–12, of what happened before the horses came;
- how long it was before the survivors lost all traces of other life;
- why the poet chose this number of days.

Paragraph 3 — Include:

- what it was like after the first week, lines 12–15;
- how the survivors would behave if the radios should start to work again, and why they would behave that way;
- some details of the poet's description of the nuclear attack in lines 19–20, and why this is a good description — quote / explain / comment;
- how the poet describes the tractors lying unused in the fields and why this is a good comparison — quote / explain / comment.

Paragraph 4 — Include:

- how the poet helps us to imagine the sound of the horses coming nearer and nearer — quote / explain / comment;
- how he describes the horses in lines 39–41 and why this is a good comparison — quote / explain / comment;
- how the people treat the horses, lines 46–47 — quote / explain / comment.

Paragraph 5 — Conclusion — include:

- whether you feel the poem has a happy or an unhappy ending;
- what makes the ending happy or unhappy;
- whether you enjoyed reading the poem;
- any features or parts of the poem you particularly liked;
- whether the poem made you think about any aspect of life;
- one sentence summing up your final impression of the poem.

HORSES

1.

Those lumbering horses in the steady plough,
On the bare field — I wonder why, just now,
They seemed terrible, so wild and strange,
Like magic power on the stony grange.

2.

Perhaps some childish hour has come again,
When I watched fearful, through the blackening rain,
Their hooves like pistons in an ancient mill
Move up and down, yet seem as standing still.

3.

Their conquering hooves which trod the stubble down
Were ritual that turned the field to brown,
And their great hulks were seraphim of gold,
Or mute ecstatic monsters on the mould.

4.

And oh the rapture, when, one furrow done,
They marched broad-breasted to the sinking sun!
The light flowed off their bossy sides in flakes;
The furrows rolled behind like struggling snakes.

5.

But when at dusk with steaming nostrils home
They came, they seemed gigantic in the gloam,
And warm and glowing with mysterious fire
That lit their smouldering bodies in the mire.

6.

Their eyes as brilliant and as wide as night
Gleamed with a cruel apocalyptic light.
Their manes the leaping ire of the wind
Lifted with rage invisible and blind.

7.

Ah, now it fades! it fades! and I must pine
Again for that dread country crystalline,
Where the blank field and the still-standing tree
Were bright and fearful presences to me.

Unseen Textual Analysis
Horses by Edwin Muir

All answers should be supported by close reference to the text.

This poem is based on a true incident: in his wartime diary, the poet writes of seeing horses in a field from a train sitting in a station.

1. Referring to stanza 1, lines 1–4, describe the effect that the horses have on the poet.   (2) U

2. Explain the relationship between line 5 and stanza 1.   (2) A

3. Basing your answer on information drawn from stanzas 2 to 6, lines 5–24, what kind of childhood would you say the poet had?   (2) U

4. Referring to the **first three stanzas** of the poem, lines 1–12, show how the poet suggests:
    (a) the size of the horses;   (2) A
    (b) the power / strength of the horses;   (2) A
    (c) the fabulous / legendary aspect of the horses.   (2) A

    (You may wish to refer to such techniques / devices as lexical choice, imagery, figures of speech . . .)

5. Show how the poet uses light imagery in stanzas 4 to 6, lines 13–24, to convey:
    (a) the beauty of the horses;   (3) A
    (b) the mystical / magical aspect of the horses.   (3) A

6. How appropriate is the poetic form used in this poem?   (2) A

7. To what extent do you consider the final stanza of the poem to be an effective and fitting conclusion to the poem, in terms of
    (a) structure;   (1) AE
    (b) tone;   (3) AE
    (c) theme?   (6) UE

Total Marks   (30)

Unseen Textual Analysis
Horses by Edwin Muir

This poem is based on a true incident: in his wartime diary, the poet writes of seeing horses in a field from a train sitting in a station.

1. Explain, **in your own words**, what the poet is watching, at the beginning of the poem.   (1) U

2. (a) Why do the horses make such an impression on the poet?   (1) U
   (b) Quote from the poem to support your answer at *(a)*.   (1) A

3.   *"Those lumbering horses . . .",* line 1.
   (a) What does that phrase tell you about the horses?   (2) A
   (b) Write down and explain **a phrase from stanza 3**, lines 9–12, which gives the same idea as "lumbering".   (2) A

4. (a) Write down the **simile** from stanza 2, lines 5–8.   (1) A
   (b) Explain, **in your own words**, what is being compared to what.   (1) A
   (c) What does this comparison tell us about the horses?   (1) A

5. Basing your answer on information drawn from stanzas 2–6, lines 5–24, what kind of childhood would you say the poet had?   (2) U

6. (a) How did the poet feel about horses when he was a child?   (2) U
   (b) Quote from the poem to support your answer at *(a)*.   (1) A

7. (a) Which farming process is referred to in lines 9–10?   (1) U
   (b) Why does the poet refer to this process as "ritual"?   (1) A

8.   *"And their great hulks were seraphim of gold",* line 11.
   (a) Seraphim are angels. What do you find **surprising** about this description of the horses in line 11?   (2) A
   (b) How is the idea in "seraphim of gold" continued in lines 13 – 16?   (2) A
   (c) Write down another **image**, from stanza 5, lines 17 – 20, which uses the idea of light.   (1) A
   (d) Describe, **in your own words**, the picture this image brings into your mind.   (2) A

9. (a) Which phrase in the poem do you think best presents the horses as exciting **or** strange **or** beautiful?   (1) E
   (b) Explain why you chose that phrase.   (1) AE

10.   *"Ah, now it fades! it fades! and I must pine",* line 25.
    (a) What has the poet been picturing in his mind?   (1) U
    (b) Explain why you think it was a happy **or** a sad picture.   (2) E
    (c) How does he feel when the picture fades?   (1) A

Total Marks   **(30)**

Suggestions for Critical Essays

(For general guidance on writing critical essays, see page 165.)

1. Choose a poem in which the poet puts across his views on some aspect of human life. Discuss the techniques / devices he has used to convey his ideas to you and the extent to which you consider those ideas to be reasonable.

   [This question is suitable for *Childhood*. **Use your discussion notes.**]

2. Choose a poem in which the poet's skill in the use of linguistic devices makes a significant contribution to the poem's impact and show how this skill has helped you to understand the poet's ideas and / or beliefs.
   (You may wish to deal with such aspects as imagery, lexical choice, syntax . . .)

   [This question is suitable for both *Childhood* and *The Horses*. **Use your discussion notes.**]

3. Choose a poem which tells a story and show how the poet uses the particular techniques / devices of the narrative form to put across his ideas and beliefs.

   [This question is suitable for *The Horses*. **Use your discussion notes.**]

4. Choose a poem which has an important message to convey. Explain the significance of the subject and show how the poetic devices used in the poem help to convey the importance of its theme.
   (You may wish to deal with such aspects as poetic / literary form, analogy, symbolism, imagery.)

   [This question is suitable for *The Horses*. **Use your discussion notes.**]

5. Compare and contrast two poems by the same writer, which touch on the relationship between Man and Nature, making clear in your evaluation of the techniques / devices used in the poems which one, in your opinion, puts the poet's ideas across more strongly.

   [This question is suitable for *Childhood* and *The Horses*. **Use your discussion notes for both poems.**]

Some Ideas and Suggestions for Writing

(For general guidance on writing essays for Language Study Unit, see page 168.)

1. **Muir believed that childhood was an idyllic time. Do you feel that Muir's is a realistic view of childhood or would you argue that this time of life has its pitfalls like any other?**
    (This is expressive writing: a **personal reflective** essay.)
    Beware of writing a simple, anecdotal essay about your own childhood. You may offer anecdotes from your early life as examples but the main thrust of your essay should be your reflections on the state of childhood per se. Start by making clear whether or not you agree with Muir's view of childhood. You may like to think of a framework to take you through your childhood — e.g., the family photograph album, toys you loved at a particular age . . . but make sure you reflect on the condition of childhood each time.

2. **Write about a place where you feel you belong completely.**
    (This is expressive writing: a **personal reflective** essay; or creative writing: a **poem** or set of poems.)
    This may be your own room, your family home, some organisation whose ideals you embrace wholeheartedly or some favourite spot you visit often.
    Start by describing the place, concentrating on the feeling of belonging this place inspires in you and trying to explain why you feel this way. Write about specific occasions when you have felt the comforting effect of this place, concentrating on your feelings when you approached this place and how it worked its magic on you.
    If you choose the poetry option, you might consider the place in different seasons, or when you are in a variety of moods.

3. **Scientists cloned Dolly, the sheep, and are on the verge of cloning body replacement parts for human beings, opening up the possibility of cloning complete human beings . . . Have they gone too far?**
    (This is expressive writing: a **persuasive** essay; or creative writing: a **dramatic monologue / speech**.)
    Begin by stating your opinion in answer to the question, Have they gone too far?
    The rest of your essay depends on that answer. If you answer Yes, you might start by considering the benefits of science today, compared to the past, e.g., things we take for granted like antibiotics, before going on to explain why you think scientific development is now out of control, with scientists behaving like Gods of creation . . . Your arguments will mostly be moral / ethical / religious . . . If you answer No, you will want to deal with the moral / ethical / religious arguments first, before going on to explain what you consider to be the benefits of modern scientific development.

4. **Write a short story about survivors of a nuclear attack.**
    (This is creative writing: a piece of **prose fiction**.)
    If you are a Sci Fi reader, this may be a good opportunity for you to air your knowledge of this kind of scenario but do be careful not to copy the ideas of a story you have read — you'd be surprised to know how many teachers / examiners are familiar with the genre.
    Concentrate on the impact of the attack on the survivors and how they try to pick up the pieces of civilisation and start afresh. Have they learned any lessons? Will they continue as before? A good story needs some sort of conflict: for example, not all of the characters who have survived will have the same ideas about how to proceed.

CHAPTER 4
George Mackay Brown:

Hamnavoe and *The Old Women*

GEORGE MACKAY BROWN, 1921–1996

The poet and his work

An Orcadian, like Edwin Muir, George Mackay Brown was born in Stromness on 17th October, 1921, but unlike Muir, he did not spend much time away from his beloved Orkney. His father was a tailor but, in order to support his growing family, he became a postman, continuing with the tailoring as a side-line. His mother, daughter of a crofter-fisherman, spoke Gaelic; George was the youngest of her six children, with four brothers and one sister. The first poem in this chapter, *Hamnavoe*, uses his father's postal round as a framework to present the town (Stromness) and its community; the poem ends in a sincere and moving tribute to the man who worked hard to provide him with food and shelter, whilst allowing him to grow up in a carefree, secure environment. His father was a strong socialist and a religious man with a great love of hymn-singing; both of those traits are evident in the postman in *Hamnavoe*. His maternal grandfather's twin occupations were typical of this community and they too are celebrated in *Hamnavoe*. The town itself is almost another character in the poem, presented largely as the sum of its inhabitants, with a timeless quality distilled from the continuity of generations; his own family had been in Stromness for four hundred years.

Unlike MacDiarmid, Mackay Brown did not come from a literature-oriented family. He discovered at school that he was good at writing and felt it was his vocation to use this talent. He suffered from tuberculosis at the age of 20 and his poem *Snow: from a hospital*, a reminder of that time, gives us one of the few glimpses of the poet to appear in his work. In 1951, when he was 30 years old, he went to study in Newbattle Abbey, the Adult Education College run at that time by Edwin and Willa Muir. One can see that the presence of the Muirs would be a source of great comfort to him and, indeed, in this atmosphere he blossomed: three years later, in 1954, he was able to publish his first collection of poetry, entitled *The Storm*, the title poem of which is used for the unseen textual analysis exercise in this chapter. From Newbattle, he went on to study at Edinburgh University, where he gained a second class honours degree in English Literature.

An unworldly man with no thoughts of material success, he was deeply religious, content to live the simple island life of his forebears, and very sensitive to his ancient heritage. Very many of his poems have an underlying spiritual element as he searched for the truth, preoccupied with the mystery of death and the hereafter; one of those is the second poem in this chapter: *The Old Women*, in which he begins with a picture of old women gossiping, but in the sestet of the poem, he raises those same old women to Biblical stature when faced with the death of a young fisherman. He converted to Roman Catholicism in 1961, finding comfort in the ritual and ceremony of that faith, whose God was a forgiving, understanding Father, unlike the harsh taskmaster of the Calvinists. The symbolism of the Roman Catholic faith comes through in his poems, particularly in his love of significant numbers, three for the Holy Trinity, fourteen for the Stations of the Cross; stones recall the Resurrection and every birth and death recalls the birth and death of Christ.

He is often portrayed as something of a hermit, but Peter Maxwell-Davies, the composer who fell in love with and settled in Orkney, where some of his compositions were inspired by George Mackay Brown's poetry, tells of many sociable evenings spent in George's company; although he did perhaps have the islander's wariness of strangers. His work deals with the simple life and people of his native island and, more so than Muir, he himself was the very essence of an Orcadian.

HAMNAVOE

My father passed with his penny letters
Through closes opening and shutting like legends
    When barbarous with gulls
    Hamnavoe's morning broke

5   On the salt and tar steps. Herring boats,
Puffing red sails, the tillers
    Of cold horizons, leaned
    Down the gull-gaunt tide

And threw dark nets on sudden silver harvests.
10   A stallion at the sweet fountain
    Dredged water, and touched
    Fire from steel-kissed cobbles.

Hard on noon four bearded merchants
Past the pipe-spitting pierhead strolled,
15   Holy with greed, chanting
    Their slow grave jargon.

A tinker keened like a tartan gull
At cuithe-hung doors; a crofter lass
    Trudged through the lavish dung
20   In a dream of cornstalks and milk.

In "The Arctic Whaler" three blue elbows fell,
Regular as waves, from beards spumy with porter,
    Till the amber day ebbed out
    To its black dregs.

25   The boats drove furrows homeward, like ploughmen
In blizzards of gulls. Gaelic fisher girls
    Flashed knife and dirge
    Over drifts of herring,

And boys with penny wands lured gleams
30   From the tangled veins of the flood. Houses went blind
    Up one steep close, for a
    Grief by the shrouded nets.

The kirk, in a gale of psalms, went heaving through
A tumult of roofs, freighted for heaven. And lovers
35   Unblessed by steeples, lay under
    The buttered bannock of the moon.

He quenched his lantern, leaving the last door.
Because of his gay poverty that kept
    My seapink innocence
40   From the worm and black wind;

And because, under equality's sun
All things wear now to a common soiling,
    In the fire of images
    Gladly I put my hand
45   To save that day for him.

Suggested Study Points
Hamnavoe by George Mackay Brown

Understanding

1. **The situation**
   - What is the situation presented in the poem?
   - Through whose eyes do we look, in the course of the poem?

2. **The themes**
   - **At this stage in your reading of the poem**, what themes have you noticed?
     (Don't expect to get all of them at this point!)
   - Keep adding to this list as you work through the poem.

Analysis

§1: lines 1–12
   - What do we learn about the poet's father in this section?

   - How does the poet help us to imagine what Hamnavoe is like first thing in the morning?
   - How does he immediately make us aware of the past?
   - What two ways of earning a living in the community are introduced in the first section?

   - Discuss the effectiveness of the **imagery** in the presentation of the herring boats.
   - What does it contribute to the overall impact of the poem?

   - Discuss the effectiveness of the stallion **imagery** in lines 10–12.
   - What contribution does this imagery make to the poem, as a whole?

   - Look closely at the structure and syntax in this section.
   - What are the effects of the techniques used here?
   - Look out for those techniques throughout the poem.

§2: lines 13–24
   - Discuss the effectiveness of the **imagery** in the poet's presentation of:
   - the merchants; and the old men at the pier-head;
   - the tinker; and the crofter lass;
   - the old fishermen in the pub.
   - What does each image contribute to the poem as a whole?
   - Consider the **atmosphere / mood** created in those presentations.
   - Discuss the effect of the **juxtaposition** of those images.
   - How are we made aware of time passing in this section?

§3: lines 25–36
   - Discuss the effectiveness of the **imagery** in the poet's presentation of:
   - the returning fishing boats; the fisher girls; and the boys fishing;
   - the grief in the close; the singing in the Kirk; and the lovers.
   - What does each image contribute to the poem as a whole?
   - Consider the **atmosphere / mood** created in those presentations.
   - Discuss the effect of the **juxtaposition** of those images.
   - How are we made aware of time passing in this section?

§4: lines 37–45

- What more do we learn about the poet's father in this section?
- For what things is the poet grateful to his father?

- Discuss the effectiveness of the **techniques / devices** used by the poet in the expression of his gratitude.

- Think about the meaning of lines 43–44: What is "the fire of images"?
- Discuss the effectiveness of this **metaphor** in relation to this poem.

- What feeling, as well as gratitude, do you detect in this last section?

Looking over the whole poem

- Consider the appropriateness and effectiveness of the **poetic form**.

- Discuss the overall **structure** of the poem: consider its effects and how they are achieved.

- Sum up the poet's use of **contrast** and **juxtaposition** in the poem.

- Look carefully at the **characters** introduced in the poem.
- In what way is the poet's father different from the other people mentioned?

- Can you see any religious undertones in the poem, especially in lines 37 - 45?

Evaluation

- Look over your completed list of themes dealt with in the poem.
- Some you may want to group together, as different aspects of the same theme.
- Decide if there is one main theme, or an order of priority.

- Look back on the different ways the poet has conveyed his theme(s) / attitudes to you.
- How effectively has he done so? Are some techniques more effective than others?

- The title is *Hamnavoe*; the first words are "My father . . .": a small town, a simple postman . . .
- Discuss how the poem moves beyond those simple confines to deal with human existence and the human condition.

- George Mackay Brown usually adopts a fairly objective stance in his poetry.
- In this poem, he reveals a little more of himself than usual.
- What impression have you formed of the poet from your reading of *Hamnavoe*?

- Has this poem revealed to you anything new, made you think about an area of life you had not considered before, confirmed or changed your mind about any aspect of life?

- Any other comments you would like to make about the poem?

- **Write down** one sentence summing up your final opinion of the poem.

Read the poem again quietly, to yourself, enjoy it and see how much you have gained from close study.

Using Your Notes for Revision
Hamnavoe by George Mackay Brown

Understanding and Analysis

(Use these questions to help you revise important parts of the poem.)

1. *(a)* Note the **situation** presented in *Hamnavoe*.
     (b) Note how the poet uses this situation as a framework for the poem.

2. **Look over your notes on atmosphere / mood:**
     Think about the way the poet uses **sound effects** and **contrast** to create atmosphere / mood in his descriptions of the place and its people, and the way they interconnect.

3. The poem is made up largely of a series of snapshots of the community.
     Look over your notes on the effectiveness of the devices / techniques used to create each image, and what each adds to the overall impact of the poem:
     (a) the herring boats, lines 5–9;
     (b) the stallion at the fountain, lines 10–12;
     (c) the scene on the pier, lines 13–16;
     (d) the tinker, lines 17–18;
     (e) the crofter lass, lines 18–20;
     (f)   the old fishermen in the pub, lines 21–24;
     (g) the fishing boats, lines 25–26;
     (h) the fisher girls, lines 26–28;
     (i) the boys fishing, lines 29–30;
     (j) the houses of mourning, lines 30–32;
     (k) the singing in the Kirk, lines 33–34;
     (l) the lovers, lines 34–36;
     (m) the poet as a child, lines 39–40.

Evaluation

(You might like to practise for the exam by writing an answer to this question.)

4. How effective do you think the poet has been in his use of everyday events and simple people to comment on the human condition?

     You should refer closely to the text to support each point made.   (10 marks)

     (Consult your notes on Evaluation: poem moves from one man → community → human condition.)

Using Your Notes for Revision
Hamnavoe by George Mackay Brown

Understanding and Analysis

(Use these questions to help you revise important parts of the poem.)

1. What is the poet's father doing at the beginning of the poem?

2. What is Hamnavoe like first thing in the morning?

3. *(a)* Through whose eyes do we see round the town and outlying district?
   (b) *In your own words,* describe briefly:
      (i) the other working people, and
      (ii) people who do not work, who are mentioned in the poem.

4. Explain the importance to the community of the fishing boats and the stallion.

5. **Look over your notes on the merchants in lines 13–16:**
   (a) What is the poet's, and his father's, attitude to them?
   (b) Quote from the poem to support your answer.

6. **Look over your notes on the fishing boats, especially line 9:**
   (a) What does the word "harvests" tell you about the catch?
   (b) Which occupation would you normally associate with "harvest"?
   (c) So what is the poet saying about the fishermen, by using "harvests" here?
   (d) What **two** aspects of the fish are suggested by the word "silver"?

7. **Look over your notes on the fisher girls, lines 26–28:**
   (a) What are the girls doing?
   (b) Pick out and explain **words / phrases / devices** which help to create a vivid picture of the girls.

8. **Look over your notes on the boys fishing, lines 29–30:**
   Explain why this is a good way to describe what the boys are doing and the way they feel about fishing.

Evaluation

(You might like to prepare for the exam by writing an answer to this question.)

9. *(a)* Having read this poem, what is *your impression* of Hamnavoe and the people who live there?   (7 marks)

   (You should refer to the poem to support your impressions; look over your notes on imagery.)

   (b) Would this way of life appeal to you? Why / why not?   (3 marks)

Critical Response Guide
Hamnavoe by George Mackay Brown

Paragraph 1 — Introduction — include:
- title and poet's name;
- what the poet's father is doing at the beginning of the poem;
- what Hamnavoe is like first thing in the morning; what he hears and sees.

Paragraph 2 — Include:
- through whose eyes we see round the town and outlying district;
- a brief description *in your own words*, of:
  (i)   the other working people, and
  (ii)   people who do not work, who are mentioned in the poem;
- the importance to the community of the fishing boats and the stallion.

Paragraph 3 — Include:
- more detailed description of the **merchants** in lines 13–16;
- what you think is the poet's, and his father's, **attitude** to the merchants;
- quotations from the poem to support your opinion;
- why you think this.

Paragraph 4 — Include:
- more detailed description of any two of the groups who do not work;
- the poet's, and his father's, **attitude** to them;
- quotations from the poem;
- why you think this.

Paragraph 5 — *Fishing is the main occupation mentioned in the poem.*
- Discuss some of the ways the poet describes the **herring boats** in action.
- Quote and explain some good words / phrases / devices which help you to picture them in your mind.

He also mentions the fisher girls who clean the fish and he describes boys fishing with rods.
- Discuss the poet's descriptions of the **fisher girls** and of the **boys fishing**.
- Quote and explain some good words / phrases, which help you to picture them in your mind.

Paragraph 6 — Conclusion — include:
- your impression of Hamnavoe and the people who live there, from your reading of this poem;
- why this way of life would / would not appeal to you;
- one sentence summing up your final impression of the poem.

THE OLD WOMEN

Go sad or sweet or riotous with beer
Past the old women gossiping by the hour,
They'll fix on you from every close and pier
An acid look to make your veins run sour.

5   "No help," they say, "his grandfather that's dead
Was troubled by the same dry-throated curse,
And many a night he made the ditch his bed.
This blood comes welling from the same cracked source."

On every kind of merriment they frown.
10   But I have known a gray-eyed sober boy
Sail to the lobsters in a storm, and drown.
Over his body dripping on the stones
Those same old hags would weave into their moans
An undersong of terrible holy joy.

Suggested Study Points
The Old Women by George Mackay Brown

Understanding

1. **The situation**
   - What is the poem about?

2. **The themes**
   - **At this stage in your reading of the poem**, what themes have you noticed?
     (Don't expect to get all of them at this point!)
   - Keep adding to this list as you work through the poem.

Analysis

Stanza 1, lines 1–4: What is the **tone** of this stanza? How is this tone achieved?

- Identify and discuss the effectiveness of the **device** used in line 4.

- Sum up what the poet is saying, in this stanza, about the old women.

Stanza 2, lines 5–8: What is the effect of the **direct speech** used in this stanza?
   - Does it confirm or change your impression of the old women from stanza 1?

- What is meant by "troubled by the same dry-throated curse", line 6?
   - Why don't the old women say openly what they mean?
     This is an example of euphemism.
   - Discuss the euphemism in line 7.
   - What do those devices add to your impression of the old women?

- Identify and discuss the effectiveness of the **device** used in line 8.

- Add to your impression of the old women.
   - Discuss the kind of community in which they live.
- Add to your notes on **tone**.

Stanza 3, lines 9–14
- What is the grammatical function of line 9?
   - Comment on the word order of this line.
   - How does the **tone** change with this line?

- In line 10, what does the word "But" signal?
- In line 11, what is the effect of the comma after "storm"?

- What are the **connotations** of "hags" in line 13? What is the effect of this word here?
   - Identify and discuss the effectiveness of the **device** used in this line.
   - In what way does this device add to the idea in "hags"?
   - How does the word "moans" fit in to the picture?
- Identify and discuss the effectiveness of the **device** used in line 14.

- Try to work out the **symbolic** aspect of lines 12–14.

- Has your impression of the old women changed now?

Looking over the whole poem

- Discuss the **poetic form** used in this poem.
- Look at the way the poem is laid out: is it regular or irregular?
- Is there any rhyme or metrical pattern?
- If so, note and account for any variations in the pattern.
- Find out, if you do not already know, the name given to this form.

- Has the poet made effective use of this poetic form?
- Consider his use of **contrast**, **lexical choice** and **syntax** in conjunction with the form.

Evaluation

- Look over your completed list of themes dealt with in the poem.
- Some you may want to group together, as different aspects of the same theme.
- Decide if there is one main theme, or an order of priority.

- Look back on the different ways the poet has conveyed his theme(s) / attitudes to you.
- How effectively has he done so? Are some techniques more effective than others?

- The poem is ostensibly about old women.
- Discuss how the poem moves beyond those particular women, to deal with the broader themes.

- Has this poem revealed to you anything new, made you think about an area of life you had not considered before, confirmed or changed your mind about any aspect of life?

- Any other comments you would like to make about the poem?

- **Write down** one sentence summing up your final opinion of the poem.

Read the poem again quietly, to yourself, enjoy it and see how much you have gained from close study.

> ## Using Your Notes for Revision
> ### *The Old Women* by George Mackay Brown

Understanding and Analysis

(Use these questions to help you revise important parts of the poem.)

1. **Look over your notes on the old women in stanzas 1 and 2:**
   What impression does the poet create of the old women and of the kind of community in which they live?

2. **Revise your notes on the effectiveness of the devices / techniques** used by the poet in the first two stanzas, to bring the old women to life on the page.

3. **Look over your notes on tone:**
   (a) Identify and account for the tone of the first two stanzas, lines 1–8.
   (b) Identify and account for the change in tone in the third stanza, lines 9–14;
   (c) Revise the effectiveness of the techniques / devices used to bring about this change.

Evaluation

(You might like to practise for the exam by writing an answer to this question.)

4. Consider your personal response to the old women in the first stanza, and show how the focus of your response changes as the poet uses the old women to make a statement of universal significance. (10 marks)

   (Think of the way the poet presents the old women in stanza 3, as part of the religious symbolism in that stanza. If you do not already know, find out about the function of the Chorus in Greek drama.)

Using Your Notes for Revision
The Old Women by George Mackay Brown

Understanding and Analysis

(Use these questions to help you revise important parts of the poem.)

1. *(a)* Who are the old women mentioned in the title?
    (b) What does the poet say about them in stanza 1?

2. Why do the old women refer to "his grandfather" in stanza 2?

3. What can you gather from stanzas 1 and 2 about the kind of place where the poet and the old women live?

4. **Find, and make sure you understand**, the expression from stanza 1, which describes the effect those old women can have on you.

5. **Revise your notes on the effectiveness of the techniques / devices** used by the poet in stanzas 1 and 2, to help us to imagine what the old women are like.

6. **Look over your notes on tone:**
    (a) In stanzas 1 and 2, what do you think the poet's **attitude** to the old women is? Find evidence from the poem to justify your answer.
    (b) Make sure you understand why and how the tone changes in stanza 3. Pick out some evidence from the poem to support your answer.

7. **Look over your notes on stanza 3:**
    (a) In what ways is the old women's treatment of the drowned boy different from the way they treat the boy in stanzas 1 and 2?
    (b) Why do they treat the drowned boy differently?

8. **Revise your notes on the religious symbolism** in stanza 3.

Evaluation

(You might like to practise for the exam by writing an answer to this question.)

9. *(a)* What was your personal response to the old women in stanzas 1 and 2?   (3 marks)
    (b) To what extent do you find that your reaction to them has changed at the end of stanza 3? (Give reasons for your change of attitude towards them.)   (7 marks)

Critical Response Guide
The Old Women by George Mackay Brown

Paragraph 1 — Introduction — Include:

- title and poet's name;
- who the old women mentioned in the title are;
- what the poet says about them in stanza 1;
- quote and explain the expression from stanza 1 which describes the effect those old women can have on you.

Paragraph 2 — Explain:

- why the old women refer to "his grandfather" in stanza 2;
- the **techniques / devices** which the poet uses in stanza 2 to help us to imagine what the old women are like;
- what you can gather from stanzas 1 and 2 about the kind of place where the poet and the old women live.

Paragraph 3 — Explain:

- the poet's **attitude** to the old women in stanzas 1 and 2;
- evidence from the poem to justify your opinion;
- why and how the **tone** of the poem changes in stanza 3.

Paragraph 4 — Explain:

- how the old women treat the drowned boy in stanza 3;
- the religious **symbolism** in this stanza.

Paragraph 5 — Conclusion — include:

- your personal response to the old women in stanzas 1 and 2;
- the extent to which you find that your reaction to them has changed at the end of poem;
- reasons for your change of attitude;
- one sentence summing up your final impression of the poem.

THE STORM

What blinding storm there was! How it
Flashed with a leap and lance of nails,
      Lurching, O suddenly
      Over the lambing hills,

5   Hounding me there! With sobbing lungs
I reeled past kirk and alehouse
      And the thousand candles
      Of gorse round my mother's yard,

And down the sand shot out my skiff
10   Into the long green jaws, while deep
      In summer's sultry throat
      Dry thunder stammered.

Swiftly the sail drew me over
The snarling Sound, scudding before
15   The heraldic clouds now
      Rampant all around.

The sea — organ and harps — wailed miserere;
Swung me in fluent valleys, poised
      On icy yielding peaks
20   Hissing spume, until

Rousay before me, the stout mast
Snapped, billowing down helpless sail.
      What evil joy the storm
      Seized us! plunged and spun!

25   And flung us, skiff and man (wave-crossed, God-lost)
On a rasp of rock! . . . The shore breakers,
      Stained chancel lights,
      Cluster of mellow bells,

Crossed hands, scent of holy water . . .
30   The storm danced over all that night,
      Loud with demons, but I
      Safe in Brother Colm's cell.

Next morning in tranced sunshine
The corn lay squashed on every hill;
35   Tang and tern were strewn
      Among the highest pastures.

I tell you this, my son: after
That Godsent storm, I find peace here
      These many years with
40   The Gray Monks of Eynhallow.

> ## Unseen Textual Analysis
> ### *The Storm* by George Mackay Brown

All answers should be supported by close reference to the text.

1. Describe the situation presented in the poem.   (2) U

2.
   > *". . . How it*
   > *Flashed with a leap and lance of nails,*
   > *Lurching, O suddenly"*   lines 1–3

   By particular reference to the **language** used by the poet in these lines, show how he conveys the force of the storm on land, in stanzas 1 and 2.   (4) A

3. Referring closely to examples from lines 9–26, show how the poet evokes the **sounds** of the storm at sea, and uses those sounds to mirror the man's emotions.   (5) A

4. From a close examination of lines 10–25, show how the poet creates a vivid picture of the magnitude and the violence of the storm at sea, building up to a climax as he is cast ashore.
   (You may wish to refer to such aspects as ideas, imagery, lexical choice, syntax, enjambment . . .)   (5) A

5. How does the poet create an **atmosphere / mood** of peace and tranquillity from line 26 to the end of the poem?   (5) A

6. How effective do you find the last stanza, lines 37–40, as a conclusion to the poem:
   (a) on the superficial level of the narrative;   (2) UE
   (b) as the resolution of the poem's deeper meaning?   (7) UE

Total Marks   **(30)**

Unseen Textual Analysis
The Storm by George Mackay Brown
---

1. Explain briefly what the poem is about. (1) U

2. Write down *two* pieces of evidence, from stanza 2, lines 5–8, which indicate where the speaker is at the beginning of the poem. (2) U

3.   *". . . a leap and lance of nails,"* line 2

    (a) What exactly do you think the poet is referring to in these words? (2) A
    (b) What does the word "leap" tell you about the storm? (2) A
    (c) Try to explain the **effect** of the words "lance" and "nails". (2) A

4.   *". . . the long green jaws . . ."* line 10

    (a) What is the poet describing in the above phrase? (1) A
    (b) Try to explain why this is a good description. (2) A

5. Pick out and explain *three separate words* from lines 13–20, which convey the **sound** of the storm. (3) A

6. (a) Pick out and explain *two separate words* from lines 21–24, which show the force with which the boat was wrecked. (2) A
    (b) Write down and explain *two separate words* from lines 25–26, which show the violence with which the boat was cast ashore. (2) A

7. How does the poet create an **atmosphere of peace and calm** from line 26 to the end of the poem? (2) A

8. What do we find out about the speaker in the last stanza? (2) U

9. (a) Do you think the story of the speaker's experience in the storm has a **happy or a sad ending**? (1) E
    (b) What makes the ending happy / sad? (2) E

10. *Think about the violent storm which the speaker experienced and where he ended up.*
    (a) What do you think the **symbolic** meaning of the storm might be? (2) U
    (b) Explain how the poet's description of the storm has helped you to appreciate the symbolic meaning of the poem. (2) UE

Total Marks **(30)**

Suggestions for Critical Essays

(For general guidance on writing critical essays, see page 165.)

1. Many poems depend for their success on the poet's skill in employing the devices of poetry. Choose a poem in which more than one poetic device contributes significantly to its impact and show how the use of such devices helped you to understand the ideas in the poem.

   (You may like to consider such aspects as imagery, lexical choice, point of view, contrast, and any other literary or linguistic techniques, which the poet has used effectively.)

   (This question is suitable for *Hamnavoe* and also for the unseen poem, *The Storm*, if you have studied it closely. **Use your discussion notes**.)

2. Many memorable poems leave the reader with a powerful impression of a person, a place or an era. Using a poem which has left you with such an impression, explain what techniques / devices are used by the poet to convey this impression.

   (This question is suitable for *Hamnavoe*. **Use your discussion notes**.)

3. By looking closely at a poem written in a particular literary form . . ., Sonnet, Dramatic Monologue, Ballad . . ., consider to what extent its particular techniques enhance the impact of the subject matter.

   (This question is suitable for *The Old Women*. **Use your discussion notes.**)

4. By referring closely both to the ideas and to the poetic techniques / devices used in a poem which you know well, show whether your appreciation of the poem depends more on the ideas or on the techniques / devices.

   (This question is suitable for *The Old Women* and also for the unseen poem *The Storm* if you have studied it closely.)

Some Ideas and Suggestions for Writing

(For general guidance on writing essays for Language Study unit, see page 168.)

1. **Write about a place that you know well, where the surroundings and the lifestyle are very different from your own.**
   (This is expressive writing: a **personal reflective** essay.)
   *Note: you are asked to write about the appearance of the place **and** what life is like there; your essay should be fairly equally divided between the two.*
   *You may choose a very remote, rural area; a sea-side resort; a very large metropolis like London or New York; a foreign place . . . **Throughout your essay**, you should be trying to bring out, reflect and comment on the contrast between your own home area and lifestyle, and those of the place you have chosen.*

2. **Discuss the relative advantages and disadvantages of living in a town and in a more remote country area. On balance, which do you prefer?**
   (This is expressive writing: an **argumentative** essay; or creative writing: a **dramatic script** or **monologue / speech**.)
   Make notes on the good and bad points of each. Decide on specific aspects which apply to both areas, e.g., facilities; compare and contrast as appropriate. Try to balance the remaining aspects of the two areas against each other. If you are left with some aspects which cannot be set against each other, deal with those in your less-preferred area first so that you can lead from your penultimate paragraph into your conclusion which should state a firm preference; if there is one aspect which clinches the choice for you, keep it for your conclusion.

3. **Write about the death of a young person, which made a strong impression on you, and reflect on your feelings and reactions at the time, as well as any changes in your ideas, attitudes or outlook, as a result of this experience.**
   (This is expressive writing: a **personal reflective** essay; or creative writing: a **poem** or set of poems.)
   You may interpret this question as experiencing a personal loss, hearing about the death from someone else or through the media; it should be about the death of someone like yourself: for example, writing about the death of Princess Diana would not be appropriate.
   Do not spend too much time recalling the circumstances of the death; the greater part of your essay should be taken up with reflection on how the experience has affected you. Consider your immediate reactions and how you eventually came to terms with this death, if personal; the thoughts, provoked by this experience, on death, life, mortality, carpe diem (seize the day); perhaps it has affected your attitude to others, family, friends . . .

4. **Adopting a persona, write your thoughts and observations as you are tossed about in a storm at sea.**
   (This is creative writing: a piece of **prose** fiction.)
   Think about your persona first: you may be male or female in any period of history. You will then be able to work out the reason for your journey, the type of craft you are sailing, the stretch of water you are crossing and the possible outcome. The quality of language in your description of the storm will be important. You may write it as a monologue or in stream of consciousness style; it could be an entry or entries in a journal, but it should be written in grammatically-correct, continuous prose.

CHAPTER 5

Iain Crichton Smith:

Old Woman and *Iolaire*

IAIN CRICHTON SMITH: 1928–1998

The poet and his work

Iain Crichton Smith was another islander, this time from Lewis, but, unlike George Mackay Brown, he spent his life trying to free himself from the religious and cultural influences of his Hebridean background. Although actually born in Glasgow, he was taken to Lewis, his mother's native island, at the age of two, his father, a merchant seaman, having died of TB when the poet was a year old.

His mother struggled to raise her children on very little money but, in the island community, they were never destitute and retained a certain dignity and a sense of tradition. The poet knew intimately the subjects of his many island poems and, while he rejected their beliefs and way of living, he did understand them and even admired their tenacity in the face of great hardship, as, for example, the circumstances which prevail in *Old Woman*, the first poem in the chapter. Several of his poems feature old women and there is something of his mother in each one.

Christina Campbell, the poet's mother, was a fisher girl, following the trawlers to far off ports to process the catch as it was landed; the poet mentions her reddened hands in several poems as a symbol of the hard life she led and he compares them to the "paler hands" of his own softer existence as schoolteacher and poet, for example, in Y*ou Lived in Glasgow*, the unseen poem in this chapter. His rejection of her culture and beliefs as he proceeded through the various stages of his education on the mainland set up a lifelong dichotomy in the poet's psyche; the "black figure" of his mother hovered over his success as a poet, silent judge of his accomplishments.

The main target of his disapproval was the Calvinist faith of which his mother was a strong adherent. His rejection of Calvinism pervades his poetry and is a major theme of both poems in this chapter. In *Iolaire*, which deals with a true incident which happened off Stornoway exactly 9 years before he was born, the poet explores the effect such an event might have on the islanders' Calvinist faith. The poem perhaps tells us more about his own response to the situation and may require some suspension of disbelief to accept it as the reaction of an elder of the Calvinist church. Calvinists are always represented in his work as black figures, like the elder in *Iolaire* and his mother in *You Lived in Glasgow*, a symbol of their negation of joy and of anything as apparently trivial as writing poetry. His *Poem of Lewis* opens with the words:*"Here they have no time for the finer graces of poetry . . ."* And to make things worse, he wrote in English! He thought that, by forsaking the Gaelic of his upbringing, he could escape the narrow, island community of his childhood, but, as the saying goes: You can take the boy out of Lewis but. . . . He felt guilty at this desertion of his mother's culture, a feeling which comes across in many poems, notably in *You'll Take a Bath*, in which he recalls visiting her in Dumbarton, when she would try to delay his departure. After his mother's death in 1969, he felt both liberated and constrained by those guilt feelings and the gap, which he could not now bridge. But his guardian angel was waiting in the wings . . .

In 1977, he married Donalda, with whom he lived very happily until his death in October, 1998. His last collection, *The Leaf and the Marble*, dedicated to Donalda "with love and gratitude" and using a holiday in Italy with her as its framework, deals with the familiar themes of the limitations of island existence and the unforgiving hold of cultural and emotional ties, but moves into an optimistic escape from those constraints through love. Sadly, we shall have no more from the pen of this great poet, but his admirers will be consoled by the resolution and harmonious melody of his swan song.

OLD WOMAN

And she, being old, fed from a mashed plate
as an old mare might droop across a fence
to the dull pastures of its ignorance.
Her husband held her upright while he prayed

5   to God who is all-forgiving to send down
some angel somewhere who might land perhaps
in his foreign wings among the gradual crops.
She munched, half dead, blindly searching the spoon.

Outside, the grass was raging. There I sat
10   imprisoned in my pity and my shame
that men and women having suffered time
should sit in such a place, in such a state

and wished to be away, yes, to be far away
with athletes, heroes, Greek or Roman men
15   who pushed their bitter spears into a vein
and would not spend an hour with such decay.

'Pray God,' he said, 'we ask you, God,' he said.
The bowed back was quiet. I saw the teeth
tighten their grip around a delicate death.
20   And nothing moved within the knotted head

but only a few poor veins as one might see
vague wishless seaweed floating on a tide
of all the salty waters where had died
too many waves to mark two more or three.

Suggested Study Points
Old Woman by Iain Crichton Smith

Understanding

1. **The situation**
   - What does the poem tell us about the old woman?

2. **The themes**
   - **At this stage in your reading of the poem**, what themes have you noticed?
     (Don't expect to get all of them at this point!)
   - Keep adding to this list as you work through the poem.

Analysis

Stanza 1, lines 1–4
- What details of the old woman's condition are we given in stanza 1?
- What impression of the old woman does the poet convey through **lexical choice** and **imagery**?
- For what do you think the husband prayed (line 4)?
- What **tone** is set in the first three words of the poem?
- What is the effect of this tone?
- What is the poet's **mood** in this stanza?

Stanza 2, lines 5–8
- What is the effect of the **enjambment** here?
- What **tone** can you detect in lines 5–6?
- Explain why the poet adopts this tone.
- Why do you think the angel is referred to as "foreign" (line 7)?
- What meaning is conveyed by the word "gradual" in line 7?
- Add to your impression of the old woman from line 8.

Stanza 3, lines 9–12
- How does the focus of the poem change in stanza 3?
- What **contrasts** are introduced here?
- Identify and explain the effectiveness of the **poetic device** used in line 9.
- What is the poet's **mood** in this stanza? What makes him feel this way?
- What **poetic devices** are used to intensify both the poet's mood and the situation he witnesses?

Stanza 4, lines 13–16
- What is the effect of the **enjambment** here?
- Where did the poet wish to be and why? Why can't he go? *(The previous stanza will help.)*
- What **poetic device** is used to intensify his desire?
- Discuss the possible **ambiguity** of the phrase "wished to be away".

- Identify and discuss the effectiveness of the **poetic device** used in line 15.
- What is the poet suggesting in stanzas 3 and 4?
- How would the old couple he is visiting react to this suggestion?

Stanza 5, lines 17–20

- Discuss the effect of the **direct speech** used in line 17.
- Identify and discuss the effectiveness of the **poetic device** used in line 17.
- What is the effect of "said" rather than a more emotive word like begged or pleaded?

- Discuss the effectiveness of the **image** of the old man presented in line 18.
- What is the effect of the **caesura**?
- Discuss the effectiveness of the **image** of the old woman in lines 18–19.

Stanza 6, lines 21–24

- Discuss the effectiveness of the **image** of the old woman, started in line 20.

- What is the effect of the **enjambment** here?

- Discuss the effectiveness of the **metaphor** in the last two lines of the poem.

- Discuss the poet's mood at the end of the poem.

Looking over the whole poem

- Consider the appropriateness and effectiveness of the **poetic form** used in this poem.

- What is the effect of having no definite or indefinite article in the title?

Evaluation

- Look over your completed list of themes dealt with in the poem.
- Some you may want to group together, as different aspects of the same theme.
- Decide if there is one main theme or an order of priority.

- Look back on the different ways the poet has conveyed his theme(s) / attitudes to you.
- How effectively has he done so? Are some techniques more effective than others?

- Discuss how the poem moves beyond one old woman to deal with human existence and the human condition.

- What impression have you formed of the poet from your reading of *Old Woman*?

- Has this poem revealed to you anything new, made you think about an area of life you had not considered before, confirmed or changed your mind about any aspect of life?

- Any other comments you would like to make about the poem?

- **Write down** one sentence summing up your final opinion of the poem.

Read the poem again quietly, to yourself, enjoy it and see how much you have gained from close study.

Using Your Notes for Revision
Old Woman by Iain Crichton Smith

Understanding and Analysis

(Use these questions to help you revise important parts of the poem.)

1.   Summarise, in your own words, details of the old woman and her situation.

2.   **Look over your notes on the poet's presentation of the old woman**:
Revise the effectiveness of the **poetic devices / techniques**, which have helped to form your impression of the old woman and her situation.

(You should have notes on lexical choice, simile, metaphor, alliteration, repetition and perhaps also hypallage, enjambment, ambiguity and euphemism.)

3.   **Look over your notes on mood**:
(a)   Trace the changes in mood and tone throughout the poem;
(b)   make sure you have evidence of the reasons for the poet's feelings;
(c)   note how you are made aware of each mood change.

(Consult your notes on contrast, pathetic fallacy, alliteration, repetition and synecdoche.)

Evaluation

(You might like to practise for the exam by writing an answer to this question.)

4.   *(a)*   Explain the importance to the poem of lines 14 and 15:
    "with athletes, heroes, Greeks or Roman men
    who pushed their bitter spears into a vein"   (5 marks)

(Think of the idea suggested in line 15 and the effect of introducing classical references.)

   (b)   **Referring closely to the whole poem**, discuss the extent to which you agree with the ideas expressed in those lines.   (5 marks)

(A personal response to the ideas in the poem is required here but remember to base your response on the situation presented in the poem.)

Level: Intermediate 1

Using Your Notes for Revision
Old Woman by Iain Crichton Smith

Understanding and Analysis

1.   Summarise, in your own words, details of the old woman and her situation.

2.   *"as an old mare might droop across a fence*
                        to the dull pastures of its ignorance."   lines 2–3
      (a)   To what is the old woman compared in those lines?
      (b)   Pick out two details about the old woman from **stanza 1**, which justify this comparison.
      (c)   What is the poet saying about the old woman by making this comparison?

3.   What do you think the husband asks God to do in lines 4–6?

4.   *"Outside the grass was raging."*   line 9
      (a)   Is the grass really raging? What does the poet mean by that sentence?
      (b)   What other feelings does the poet express in this stanza in lines 9–12?
      (c)   Why does he have those feelings?

5.   *"'Pray God,' he said, 'we ask you, God,' he said.*
                        The bowed back was quiet. . . ."   lines 17–18
      (a)   What two **techniques / devices** does the poet use in line 17 to help us hear the old man's prayer in our minds?
      (b)   Explain the **device** used in line 18, which helps us to picture what the old man looks like as he prays.

6.   *"And nothing moved within the knotted head*

                        but only a few poor veins as one might see
                        vague wishless seaweed floating on a tide" lines 20–22
      (a)   Note two details of the old woman's appearance, mentioned in those lines.
      (b)   What does the poet compare to seaweed?
      (c)   Explain why this is a good comparison.

Evaluation

(You might like to practise for the exam by writing an answer to this question.)

7.   *"with athletes, heroes, Greek or Roman men*
                        who pushed their bitter spears into a vein"   lines 14–15
      (a)   Explain, in your own words, what those Greek or Roman heroes did.   (2 marks)
      (b)   What is the poet suggesting in those lines, in relation to the old woman?   (3 marks)
      (c)   To what extent do you agree with the poet's idea expressed here?   (5 marks)
            (You should refer to the poem to justify your answer.)

Critical Response Guide
Old Woman by Iain Crichton Smith

Paragraph 1 — Introduction — include:
- title and poet's name;
- description, in your own words, of the old woman and her situation;
- what you think the husband asked God to do.

Paragraph 2 — Include:
- what the old woman is compared to in stanza 1;
- two details about the old woman from the first stanza which justify this comparison;
- details from line 10 also supporting the Simile in stanza 1;
- what the poet is saying about the old woman by making this comparison.

Paragraph 3 — Describe and explain:
- what is meant by "Outside the grass was raging." in line 9;
- other feelings which the poet expresses in this stanza, lines 9–12;
- why he has those feelings.

Paragraph 4 — Explain:
- how the poet gets our sympathy for the old man as well as for his wife;
- quote / comment on the **two** techniques / devices which the poet uses in line 17 to help us hear the old man's prayer in our minds;
- the **device** in line 18 which helps us to picture what the old man looks like as he prays.

Paragraph 5 — Include:
- how the poet describes the old woman in the last two stanzas:
- how he shows her as being close to death;
- two details of her appearance in lines 20–21;
- seaweed comparison in line 22 — quote / explain / comment.

Paragraph 6 — Explain:
- what the poet is saying about God in the last two lines of the poem;
- how the poet is feeling at the end of the poem.

Paragraph 7 — Conclusion — include:
- why the poet mentions Greek and Roman heroes in lines 14–15;
- what those Greek or Roman heroes did;
- what the poet is suggesting in those lines in relation to the old woman;
- whether you agree with the poet's idea expressed here;
- a final sentence summing up your opinion of the poem.

IOLAIRE

The poem tells the story of a real event. In the early hours of New Year's morning, 1919, the Admiralty yacht *Iolaire* was wrecked in a rough sea on the Beasts of Holm, just outside Stornoway harbour. She left Kyle about 8pm, carrying 260 Royal Navy ratings, who were looking forward to bringing in the first peaceful New Year with their families, in many cases the first time they had been together since the beginning of World War I, four and a half years earlier. An elder of the Calvinist Church surveys the scene:

The green washed over them. I saw them when
the New Year brought them home. It was a day
that orbed the horizon with an enigma.
It seemed that there were masts. It seemed that men
5　buzzed in the water round them. It seemed that fire
shone in the water which was thin and white
unravelling towards the shore. It seemed that I
touched my fixed hat which seemed to float and then
the sun illumined fish with naval caps,
10　names of the vanished ships. In sloppy waves,
in the fat of water, they came floating home
bruising against their island. It is true,
a minor error can inflict this death.
That star is not responsible. It shone
15　over the puffy blouse, the flapping blue
trousers, the black boots. The seagull swam
bonded to the water. Why not man?
The lights were lit last night, the tables creaked
with hoarded food. They willed the ship to port
20　in the New Year which would erase the old,
its errant voices, its unpractised tones.
Have we done ill, I ask, my fixed body
a simulacrum of the transient waste,
for everything was mobile, plants that swayed,
25　the keeling ship exploding and the splayed
cold insect bodies. I have seen your church
solid. This is not. The water pours
into the parting timbers where I ache
above the globular eyes. The slack heads turn
30　ringing the horizon without sound,
with mortal bells, a strange exuberant flower
unknown to our dry churchyards. I look up.
The sky begins to brighten as before,
remorseless amber, and the bruised blue grows
35　at the erupting edges. I have known you, God,
not as the playful one but as the black
thunderer from hills. I kneel
and touch this dumb blond head. My hand is scorched.
Its human quality confuses me.
40　I have not felt such hair so dear before
nor seen such real eyes. I kneel from you.
This water soaks me. I am running with
its tart sharp joy. I am floating here
in my black uniform. I am embraced
45　by these green ignorant waters. I am calm.

Suggested Study Points
Iolaire by Iain Crichton Smith

Understanding

1. The situation
- What does the poem tell us about the events on that New Year's morning?
- Who is speaking in the poem, and to whom?

2. The themes
- **At this stage in your reading of the poem**, what themes have you noticed?
  (Don't expect to get all of them at this point!)
- Keep adding to this list as you work through the poem.

Analysis

§1: lines 1–12
- What **tone** and **mood** are set in the first 5 lines of the poem?
- Discuss the syntactical and poetic devices used to make this tone / mood clear to you.

- What is the "enigma" referred to in line 3? *(Make sure you know what the word means!)*
- How is the idea of "enigma" continued in lines 4–8?
- What is the speaker's **mood** in those lines?

- Identify and discuss the effectiveness of the **image** in lines 4–5.
- Discuss the effectiveness of the poet's **lexical choice** in line 7.
- Consider the layers of meaning in "my fixed hat" in line 8.
- Discuss the **image** in lines 9–10.
- Discuss the **lexical choice** in lines 10–12.
- What **mood** is indicated here?

§2: lines 12–21: How does the poet set up an immediate **contrast** in this section?
- What is the **tone** here?

- What is / was the "minor error" in line 13? What do you understand by "star", line 14?
- Clarify the **contrast** between those two.
- What is the effect of the **caesura** in line 14?

- Discuss the **image** presented in lines 14–16.
- Pay attention to the **lexical choice** in those lines.
- Discuss the seagull **image** in lines 16–17.
- What **poetic device** adds to the impact of the image?
- Explain the **irony** implicit in the question in line 17. What is the speaker's **mood** here?

- Discuss the presentation of the preparations being made for the sailors' return.
- Consider the effectiveness of all of the **poetic devices** used here.
- What were the expectations of the islanders and of the returning men?
- Clarify the **irony** of the situation and the speaker's **mood**.

§3: lines 22–26
- What is the **tone** of the question in line 22? How is the tone made clear to you?

- Discuss the contrasting **images** of movement and stillness in lines 22–26.
- Consider the **metaphorical** aspect of those images. *(Discuss "simulacrum", line 23)*
- Discuss the effectiveness of the **image** in lines 25 – 26.
- Look for a link back to an earlier image.

§4: lines 26–32
- To whom are the first two sentences in this section addressed?
- What is the **tone** of his address? How is this tone achieved?
- What **contrast** is continued in those lines? What is the effect of the **syntax**?

- Discuss the effectiveness of the **image** in lines 27–29.
- What is happening to the speaker here? What are his feelings?
- Discuss the effectiveness of the **image** presented in lines 29–32.

§5: lines 32–37
- Discuss the **mood** of the speaker in this section.
- What does he mean by "the playful one" in line 36?
- Discuss the effectiveness of "the black / thunderer from hills", lines 36–37.
- Consider the effect of the line layout on the impact of this phrase.

§6: lines 37–45
- What is the significance of the speaker's action in lines 37–38?
- What effect does this action have on him? *(What feelings does he discover in himself?)*
- What is the **tone** of those lines? What decision has the speaker made in line 41?
- Look closely at lines 42–45: What do you think happens in the end?
- Discuss the devices / techniques used to give those lines added impact.

Looking over the whole poem
- Examine the **poetic form** used in this poem. Is it appropriate to the sense of the poem?
- To what extent has the poet used it effectively?

Evaluation

- Look over your completed list of themes dealt with in the poem.
- Some you may want to group together as different aspects of the same theme.
- Decide if there is one main theme or an order of priority.
- Look back on the different ways the poet has conveyed his theme(s) / attitudes to you.
- How effectively has he done so? Are some techniques more effective than others?

- Discuss the effectiveness of the poet's use of a **persona** in this poem.

- Has this poem revealed to you anything new, made you think about an area of life you had not considered before, confirmed or changed your mind about any aspect of life?

- **Write down** one sentence summing up your final opinion of the poem.

Read the poem again quietly, to yourself, enjoy it and see how much you have gained from close study.

Using Your Notes for Revision
Iolaire by Iain Crichton Smith

Understanding and Analysis

(Use these questions to help you revise important parts of the poem.)

1.   *(a)*   Summarise what happens in the poem.

      (b)   Make sure you understand the enigma and the irony of the situation.

2.   **Look over your notes on mood and tone:**
Trace the development of **mood** and **tone** through the poet's skilful use of syntactical and poetic techniques.

(You should have notes on sentence structure, punctuation, repetition, poetic form . . .)

3.   **Look over your notes on imagery:**
Revise the effectiveness of the **imagery** used to help us picture the scene which confronts the Elder after the shipwreck.

Evaluation

(You might like to practise for the exam by writing an answer to this question.)

4.   *(a)*   The ending of the poem can be understood in two ways.
Briefly outline the two possible interpretations, giving evidence for each one from lines 42–45.   (2 marks)

          (Think along the lines of literal / metaphorical interpretations.)

      (b)   In more detail, state clearly which is your preferred ending, drawing evidence from the whole poem to support your claim.   (6 marks)

          (Consider for which side the evidence is more convincing. Think, too, about what you know of Iain Crichton Smith's beliefs – see page 89.)

      (c)   Explain how your interpretation affects the impact of the poem.   (2 marks)

          (To what extent does it support the themes of the poem?)

Using Your Notes for Revision
Iolaire by Iain Crichton Smith

Understanding and Analysis

(Use these questions to help you revise important parts of the poem.)

1. Explain what has happened at the beginning of the poem.

2. (a) Who is speaking in the poem?
   (b) Where is this person and what is he doing there?

3. **Look again at lines 4–7.**
   (a) What is being described here?
   (b) Note the details of the scene.

4. (a) What words are repeated several times in lines 4–8?
   (b) What is the effect of that repetition?
   (c) Note the words from line 12, which introduce a **contrast** to the first eleven lines of the poem.

5.   *". . . the puffy blouse, the flapping blue*
              trousers, the black boots."   lines 15–16
   (a) What is the poet describing in these lines?
   (b) What do you picture from the words "puffy blouse" and "flapping blue trousers"?
   (c) Explain why the poet uses the words "puffy" and "flapping" here.

6.   *"The lights were lit last night, the tables creaked*
              with hoarded food. They willed the ship to port"   lines 18–19
   (a) What scene is the poet describing in these lines?
   (b) Why was the food "hoarded"?
   (c) What were those people looking forward to?
   (d) What is the significance of the time of year when this event took place?

7.   *"Have we done ill, I ask . . ."*   line 22
   (a) To whom is the speaker addressing the question in line 22?
   (b) Why does he ask that question?

Evaluation

(You might like to practise for the exam by writing an answer to this question.)

8. (a) What do you think happens at the end of the poem?   (1 mark)
   (b) Give reasons / evidence for your interpretation of the ending.   (3 marks)
   (c) Why does the speaker take this action in the end?   (3 marks)
   (d) Do you approve of the speaker's final action? Why / why not?   (3 marks)

Critical Response Guide
Iolaire by Iain Crichton Smith

Paragraph 1 — Introduction — include:
- title and poet's name;
- what has happened at the beginning of the poem;
- who is speaking in the poem;
- where this person is and what he is doing there.

Paragraph 2 — Include:
- what is being described in lines 4–8;
- details of the scene *in your own words.*
- words which are repeated several times in lines 4–8;
- the effect of that **repetition**;
- words from line 12 which introduce a **contrast** to the first eleven lines;
- an explanation of the whole sentence (lines 12–14).

Paragraph 3 — Include:
- what is described in lines 15–16;
- what you imagine from the words "puffy blouse" and "flapping blue trousers";
- why the poet uses the words "puffy" and "flapping" here.

Paragraph 4 — Include:
- *in your own words*, the scene described in lines 18–20;
- why the food was "hoarded";
- what those people were looking forward to;
- the significance of the time of year when this event took place.

Paragraph 5 — Include:
- the question in line 22 (quote);
- to whom the speaker is addressing the question;
- why he asks that question.

Paragraph 6 — Explain:
- in what way the **ending** of the poem is not clear;
- what you think happens at the end of the poem;
- reasons for your interpretation of the ending;
- why the speaker takes this action in the end.

Paragraph 7 — Conclusion — Include:
- how you feel about the ending of the poem:
- whether you approve of the speaker's final action;
- why / why not;
- one sentence summing up your final impression of the poem.

'YOU LIVED IN GLASGOW'

You lived in Glasgow many years ago.
I do not find your breath in the air.
It was, I think, in the long-skirted thirties
when idle men stood at every corner
5   chewing their fag-ends of a failed culture.
Now I sit here in George Square
where the War Memorial's yellow sword glows bright
and the white stone lions mouth at bus and car.
A maxi-skirted girl strolls by.
10   I turn and look. It might be you. But no.
Around me there's a 1970 sky.

Everywhere there are statues. Stone remains.
The mottled flesh is transient. On those trams,
invisible now but to the mind, you bore
15   your groceries home to the 1930 slums.
'There was such warmth,' you said. The gaslight hums
and large caped shadows tremble on the stair.
Now everything is brighter. Pale ghosts walk
among the spindly chairs, the birchen trees.
20   In lights of fiercer voltage you are less
visible than when in winter you
walked, a black figure, through the gaslit blue.

The past's an experience that we cannot share.
Flat-capped Glaswegians and the Music Hall.
25   Apples and oranges on an open stall.
A day in the country. And the sparkling Clyde
splashing its local sewage at the wall.
This April day shakes memories in a shade
opening and shutting like a parasol.
30   There is no site for the unshifting dead.
You're buried elsewhere though your flickering soul
is a constant tenant of my tenement.

You were happier here than anywhere, you said.
Such fine neighbours helping when your child
35   almost died of croup. Those pleasant Wildes
removed with the fallen rubble have now gone
in the building programme which renews each stone.
I stand in a cleaner city, better fed,
in my diced coat, brown hat, my paler hands
40   leafing a copy of the latest book.
Dear ghosts, I love you, haunting sunlit winds,
dear happy dented ghosts, dear prodigal folk.

I left you, Glasgow, at the age of two
and so you are my birthplace just the same.
45   Divided city of the green and blue
I look for her in you, my constant aim
to find a ghost within a close who speaks
in Highland Gaelic.
                     The bulldozer breaks
50   raw bricks to powder. Boyish workmen hang
like sailors in tall rigging. Buildings sail
into the future. The old songs you sang
fade in their pop songs, scale on dizzying scale.

> # Unseen Textual Analysis
> ### *You Lived in Glasgow* by Iain Crichton Smith

All answers should be supported by close reference to the text.

Iain Crichton Smith's mother was living in Glasgow at the time of the poet's birth. The poet was alienated from his mother through his education, which took him away from the island, but more importantly encouraged him to think for himself, leading to his rejection of her Calvinist religion.

1. What can you deduce from the first verse (lines 1–11) about
    (a) the purpose of the poet's visit to Glasgow; and   (1) U
    (b) how successful this visit is?   (2) U

2.   *". . . idle men stood at every corner*
               chewing their fag-ends of a failed culture."   lines 4–5
    (a) What is your impression of the thirties from reading lines 4–5?   (1) U
    (b) Discuss the effectiveness of the language and devices used in line 5. (3) A

3. Show how the sentence structure and line layout of lines 9–10 effectively
    convey the impact made on the poet by the "maxi-skirted girl".   (2) A

4.   *"Everywhere there are statues. Stone remains.*
               The mottled flesh is transient."   lines 12–13
    (a) Discuss the effectiveness of the poet's use of contrast in these lines. (2) A
    (b) Comment on the ambiguity in "Stone remains", line 12.   (1) A
    (c) Explain the importance of the contrasting ideas in those lines in the
          context of the whole poem.   (2) UA

5.   *"There was such warmth," you said.*   line 16
    Discuss the effectiveness of three of the following techniques / devices used
    by the poet to evoke that atmosphere of "warmth" in lines 16–35:
    (a) grammatical features;
    (b) sound;
    (c) rhyme;
    (d) imagery;
    (e) lexical choice;
    (f) contrast.   (6) A

6.   *"The past's an experience that we cannot share."* line 23
    Show how this statement in line 23 is central to the main ideas raised in the
    poem, making clear the extent to which you agree with those ideas.   (10) E

                                                        Total Marks   (30)

103

Unseen Textual Analysis
You Lived in Glasgow by Iain Crichton Smith

The poet has come to Glasgow to try to recapture his memories of his mother, who was living there at the time of the poet's birth. He finds the city in which she lived has largely disappeared with the demolition of the old tenements and the appearance of multi-storey blocks of flats in their place.

1. *The poet mentions the thirties in line 3 and 1970 in line 11.*
   What is the significance of those dates in the poem?   (2) U

2. Describe, *in your own words*, your impression of city life in the thirties from lines 3–5.   (2) U

3.   *"'There was such warmth,' you said."* (line 16)
   (a) What is meant by "warmth" in the line above?   (1) U
   (b) What is the effect of using direct speech in this line?   (1) A
   (c) *Look back at the poem and find the above words in line 16.*
   How does the **rest of the line** add to the atmosphere of warmth?   (2) A

4. *Look at lines 18–21 of the poem.*
   (a) Who are the "pale ghosts" in line 18?   (1) U
   (b) What are the "lights of fiercer voltage" line 20?   (1) U
   (c) How does the word "fiercer" help to make the contrast between then and now?   (2) A
   (d) What does the poet mean by ". . . you are less / visible" in lines 20–21?   (2) U

5. (a) *In your own words*, describe the **pleasant** aspects of Glasgow, mentioned in lines 24–35.   (3) UA
   (b) What **unpleasant** aspect of the city does he mention in those lines?   (1) UA

6. (a)   *"The bulldozer breaks raw bricks to powder."*   lines 49–50
   What is the poet describing in these lines?   (1) U
   (b) Why is there a gap between "Highland Gaelic", line 48, and "The bulldozer", line 49?   (1) A

7. *Find the simile in lines 50–51.*
   (a) Explain what is compared to what in these lines.   (2) A
   (b) Why is this a good comparison? (In what ways are they alike?)   (2) A

8.   *"The past's an experience that we cannot share."* line 23
   (a) Explain, *in your own words*, what that statement means.   (2) U
   (b) To what extent do you think the poet has proved the truth of that statement in this poem? *(Refer to the poem in your answer.)*   (2) E
   (c) Do you agree with the statement? Why / why not?   (2) E

Total Marks   **(30)**

Suggestions for Critical Essays

(For general guidance on writing critical essays, see page 165.)

1. Choose a poem which has something important to say to you.
   By closely referring to the poet's language, briefly explain why you consider the subject matter to be important and go on to analyse how the language conveys the importance of the subject.
   (You may wish to consider lexical choice, syntax, imagery and any other relevant linguistic features of the poem.)

   (This question is suitable for *Old Woman*. **Use your discussion notes**.)

2. Poetry is often written as a result of reflecting on an intense emotional experience or on a significant event.

   Examine the techniques used by one poet to convey the significance of an experience or event which gave rise to a poem or sequence of poems.

   (This question is suitable for *Old Woman* or *Iolaire*. **Use your discussion notes**.)

3. Sonnet, Dramatic Monologue, Ballad . . .
   By looking closely at a poem with one such form, consider to what extent its particular techniques enhance the impact of the subject matter.

   (This question is suitable for *Iolaire*. **Use your discussion notes**.)

4. Many poems are concerned with a sense of loss or deep sadness at a particular event.
   Examine the techniques / devices by which a poet, in one poem, conveys either of those emotions to you.

   (You may wish to consider poetic form, syntax, imagery, lexical choice and any other relevant literary or linguistic features of the poem.)

   (This question is suitable for *Iolaire*. **Use your discussion notes**.)

Some Ideas and Suggestions for Writing

(For general guidance on writing essays for Language Study unit, see page 168.)

1. **If you have, or have had, an elderly relative or friend whose quality of life is poor because he / she is very frail, is suffering considerable pain and / or can no longer look after him- / herself, reflect on that person's situation and the effect on the sick person's family / friends of watching him / her suffer.**
    (This is expressive writing: a **personal reflective** essay.)
    Start by introducing the sick person, perhaps when he / she was well, able to go about and look after him- / herself, and probably others as well. Go on to contrast then and now. (Think of good ways to make the contrast, e.g., by balancing particular aspects of his / her life then and now, and by careful lexical choice.) Consider: the person's loss of dignity or his / her remarkably dignified approach to the situation, in spite of the problems; attitudes of carers, family, friends as well as the burden on those people and how they cope.
    Conclusion: how you remember / will remember the sick person after his / her death.

2. **Write an essay presenting the arguments for and against euthanasia.**
    (This is expressive writing: an **argumentative** essay.)
    Start by defining what is meant by euthanasia, and stating your position, for or against. Marshal and prioritise your arguments for and against euthanasia. Work through your evidence / reasons in detail, starting with the opposite side to your own, putting forward your arguments against those points. Go on to cite your strongest arguments for your own side, dealing with any opposing views which might be expected to arise. You may cite specific cases to support your argument, but not in any great detail. End with a really strong conclusion, restating your position.

3. **Adopting a persona, write your thoughts and observations as you regard the aftermath of a disaster.**
    (This is creative writing: a piece of **prose fiction**.)
    Do not *start by introducing yourself; your character will emerge from the thoughts and observations you express. (It is, however, essential that you think about and plan your persona before you begin.) Your character and the language he or she uses will depend on the incident you are witnessing, in terms of time and place, e.g., if your disaster is set in a different era of history; you will have to decide where your character is, e.g., in a lifeboat watching the sinking of the Titanic, hiding behind a rock witnessing the slaughter of fellow-countrymen in a great battle. You will need to know some facts about the disaster to give your writing credibility. You may choose any period in history or the future.*

4. **"Glasgow has changed . . . but not for the better."**
    Write a debating speech either supporting or opposing the above motion.
    (This is expressive writing: a **persuasive** essay; or creative writing: a **dramatic monologue / speech**.)
    Make sure you know how a debate is organised and remember that this is a speech, which should be obvious from the language used and from frequent interjections of phrases like "ladies and gentlemen", "friends", "fellow-students", etc. You may regard this as the first speech, in which case no reference will be made to the opposition, or as the second speech, in which case you may refer to points made in your opponent's speech, in order to demolish them. You will need a strong concluding sentence. It may be stating the obvious, but you will have to find out what changes have taken place in Glasgow and their effects. ("Glasgow" may be replaced in the motion by any other place or institution, e.g., your school, Scottish football or anything else you can think of.)

CHAPTER 6
Norman MacCaig:

Assisi and *Visiting Hour*

NORMAN MACCAIG, 1910–1996

The poet and his work

Norman MacCaig is the first city poet in the book. He was born in Edinburgh in 1910 and died there in 1996. He was educated at the Royal High School and the University of Edinburgh, graduating in 1932 with an honours degree in Classics. From 1932 until 1970, except for the period of the Second World War, he was involved in teaching in some capacity. He became the first Fellow in Creative Writing in his old university and later took up a permanent post as lecturer in Creative Writing at Stirling University.

In 1938, along with three other poets, he formed an avant-garde movement, the Apocalypse group, in revolt against the English political and social poetry being produced by poets like Auden in the 1930s. Norman MacCaig was one of MacDiarmid's staunchest supporters but did not follow him to the extent of writing in Scots. His first collection was published in 1945 and since then he has been a most prolific writer.

Although Edinburgh-based, MacCaig travelled abroad and his poems bear witness to that, *vide* two of the poems in this chapter, *Assisi* and *Hotel Room, 12th Floor* (New York). In his introduction to the chapter dealing with his poems in *Worlds*, he talks about an area in the north-west of Scotland, around the village of Lochinver, as being to him "the most seductive part of Scotland", and many of his poems have this rural setting. In this chapter, however, for no other reason than to balance the contents of the whole book, you will find only city-based poems, all from his later collections of the sixties. MacDiarmid accused him of failing to deal with social problems but that is certainly not true of the poems chosen for inclusion in this book. In *Assisi*, published in 1966, we see MacCaig's pity for the disabled beggar and his bitter disdain at the apathy of society and the dereliction of duty displayed by the Church. *Visiting Hour*, published in 1968, reveals equally strong feelings of pity and concern for another's plight but on a much more personal level and, while in *Assisi* his feelings were directed outwards, criticising society and the Church, in this poem he is more inclined to examine his own inner resources as he struggles to cope with a distressing experience. In the poem chosen for the unseen textual analysis, we come back to social concerns, this time in the materialistic society of New York. This later poetry is more concise and direct, the imagery less florid and often heavily laced with irony. The poems selected for this chapter, all in free verse, do not do justice to his amazing versatility, both in ideas and in form.

Norman MacCaig delighted many assemblies of school pupils with his easy manner and ready wit. He was a very sociable and popular man, not least among his fellow-writers. His 85th birthday was celebrated in Edinburgh by a gathering of friends, among them the cream of the Scottish literati, who had a great respect for the man and his accomplishments; but, sadly, by that time he was failing and he died the following year. In 1997, with the help of a grant from the Heritage Lottery Fund, his papers were acquired by Edinburgh University Library. The collection contains the poet's own copies of his books with textual alterations and revisions, as well as some 600 unpublished poems.

ASSISI

The dwarf with his hands on backwards
sat, slumped like a half-filled sack
on tiny twisted legs from which
sawdust might run,
5   outside the three tiers of churches built
in honour of St Francis, brother
of the poor, talker with birds, over whom
he had the advantage
of not being dead yet.

10   A priest explained
how clever it was of Giotto
to make his frescoes tell stories
that would reveal to the illiterate the goodness
of God and the suffering
15   of His Son. I understood
the explanation and
the cleverness.

A rush of tourists, clucking contentedly,
fluttered after him as he scattered
20   the grain of the Word. It was they who had passed
the ruined temple outside, whose eyes
wept pus, whose back was higher
than his head, whose lopsided mouth
said *Grazie* in a voice as sweet
25   as a child's when she speaks to her mother
or a bird's when it spoke
to St Francis.

Read the poem aloud, fairly slowly, and consider the following points:

1.   The title — where is Assisi?

2.   St Francis — what do you know about him?

Now you are ready to study the poem more closely.

Suggested Study Points
Assisi by Norman MacCaig

Understanding

1. **The situation**
   - What is the situation in the poem? What is happening?

2. **The themes**
   - **At this stage in your reading of the poem**, what themes have you noticed?
     (Don't expect to get all of them at this point!)
     Keep adding to this list as you work through the poem.

Analysis

Verse 1, lines 1–9
- Note, *in your own words*, the physical details in the poet's description of the beggar.

- **Tone:** Look closely at the words, phrases and comparisons used to describe the beggar.
  - How would you describe this language?
  - Note down as many examples as you can find, commenting on each example.
  - What is the effect of this language on your impression of the beggar?
  - What do you think is the poet's purpose in using such language to describe the beggar?

- lines 7–9: *". . . over whom* (St Francis) */ he had the advantage / of not being dead yet."*
  - What **tone** do you detect in these lines? *(Think of how you would say them aloud.)*
  - Consider how these lines continue the tone in lines 1–4. What does the poet mean here?
  - What do those lines tell us about the poet's feelings / attitude to the situation?

- **Irony:** *There are many examples of irony in the poem. Here is one to start you off:*
  The fact that St Francis, who loved and helped the poor, is honoured by an elaborate and costly church. Can you explain why this is ironic?

- **Juxtaposition:** *The grotesquely disabled beggar is placed* **outside** *the architecturally elaborate and beautiful church. (juxtaposition of ideas in the poem)*
  - Can you see and explain the juxtaposition in the lay-out of the lines containing these ideas in verse 1, i.e., between *(a)* the first four lines and *(b)* line five?
  - What is the effect of this juxtaposition, both in ideas and layout?
  - How is the juxtaposition helped by the **syntax** here?

- **Alliteration / Onomatopoeia:** *"sat, slumped like a half-filled sack . . . sawdust . . ."*
  - *The alliterative "s" sound suggests the sadness and pathos of the beggar's existence and is also onomatopoeic, mimicking the sound of the sawdust running out of the sack.*

- Can you see another effect of the onomatopoeia in this example?

- Find and explain the effect of another example of alliteration in this section of the poem.

Verse 2, lines 10–17
- Note the characteristics of the priest, justifying each point with evidence from the poem.

- **Tone:** lines 15–17: *"I understood / the explanation and / the cleverness."*
- What tone can be detected in these lines? Whom and / or what is the poet criticising here?

- Can you see a double meaning in the word "cleverness"? What is the effect of its position?
- How does the full stop in the middle of line 15 add to the tone?

- Explain the **irony** implicit in the priest's behaviour.

Verse 3, lines 18–27

- What are we told about the behaviour of the tourists in lines 18–21? *(2 main points here)*

- **Extended metaphor:** *"A rush of tourists . . . the Word."*, lines 18–20.
- Explain the comparison being made, noting all the words / phrases which extend the image. Discuss the effectiveness of the **metaphor**.

- Explain how the **juxtaposition** emphasises the apathy of society.
- How does the **syntax** add to the effect of the juxtaposition?

- Discuss the effectiveness of the other **devices** which you recognise in this verse.

- Add to your description of the beggar, begun in verse 1.
- Discuss the **tone** of the description and how it is achieved.

Looking over the whole poem

- Consider the appropriateness and effectiveness of the **poetic form.**

- Discuss the overall **structure** of the poem: consider its effects.

- *There are many examples of **contrast** in the poem. Here is one: **rich** tourists who can afford to take (foreign) holidays v. **poor** beggar who does not even have the means to live. The contrast intensifies the difference, thus highlighting the themes.*
- What themes are highlighted by this contrast?
- Find more examples of contrast in the poem, explain the effect of the contrast and note the theme(s) to which each one contributes.

Evaluation

- Look over your completed list of themes dealt with in the poem.
- Some you may want to group together as different aspects of the same theme.
- Decide if there is one main theme or an order of priority.

- What have you understood about the poet's attitude to the theme(s) he has presented?
- To what extent do you agree or disagree with him? Give reasons.

- Look back on the different ways the poet has conveyed his theme(s) / attitudes to you.
- How effectively has he done so? Are some techniques more effective than others?

- Has this poem revealed to you anything new, made you think about an area of life you had not considered before, confirmed or changed your mind about any aspect of life?

- Any other comments you would like to make about the poem?

- **Write down** one sentence summing up your final opinion of the poem.

Read the poem again quietly, to yourself, enjoy it and see how much you have gained from close study.

Using Your Notes for Revision
Assisi by Norman MacCaig

Understanding and Analysis

(Use these questions to help you revise important parts of the poem.)

1. Summarise the situation presented in the poem.

2. **Look over your notes on the characters:**
    Note, *in your own words*, the details of the beggar from verses 1 and 3.

3. **Look over your notes on the description of the beggar in lines 1–4:**
    (a) What kind of language is used in these lines?
    (b) Make sure you can explain all of the examples you have noted.
    (c) Note the effects of onomatopoeia and alliteration in these lines.
    (d) Comment on the tone of those lines.
    (e) What is the poet's purpose here?

4. What characteristics of the priest are suggested in verse 2?
    Make sure you have evidence from verse 2 to support each characteristic.

5. (a) What do we learn about the tourists in verse 3?
    (b) Make sure you can explain the effectiveness of the extended metaphor in lines 18–20.
    (c) What is MacCaig saying about the tourists and the priest?

6. **Look over your notes on irony:**
    (a) Make sure you can explain the irony of the situation.
    (b) Note the poet's use of contrast and juxtaposition to convey the irony and to put across the themes of the poem.

Evaluation

(You might like to practise for the exam by writing an answer to this question.)

7. Explain, in detail, and justify by close reference to the poem what you consider to be the poet's attitude to the scene he observes, making clear in your answer the extent to which you agree or disagree with him.   (10 marks)

    (Refer to your notes on tone and think of his attitude to each of the three characters / groups.)

Using Your Notes for Revision
Assisi by Norman MacCaig

Understanding and Analysis

(Use these questions to help you revise important parts of the poem.)

1. (a) Describe, *in your own words,* the main character in the poem, the beggar.
    (b) **Where exactly** does the poet see the beggar?

2. **Look over your notes on the description of the beggar in lines 1– 4:**
    (a) Note some of the words / phrases used to describe the beggar.
    (b) Explain how each word you have chosen makes the beggar seem less than human.

3   **Look over your notes on the priest in verse 2:**
    (a) What is your impression of the priest from your reading of this verse?
    (b) Make sure you have evidence to support each point.

4. **Look over your notes on the tourists in verse 3:**
    (a) To what does the poet compare the tourists in lines 18–20?
    (b) Make sure you can identify and explain the words which make up this extended metaphor.
    (c) What is MacCaig saying about the priest and the tourists in these lines?

5. **Look at your notes on the beggar in verse 3:**
    (a) What physical details can you add to your description of the beggar from this verse?
    (b) Why does the poet refer to the beggar as a "ruined temple"?
    (c) Make sure you can explain the two similes in lines 24–27.
    (d) What is he saying about the beggar in those similes?

Evaluation

(You might like to practise for the exam by writing answers to these questions.)

6. (a) What do you think the poet's feelings are towards
        (i)   the beggar?
        (ii) the priest?
        Write down some evidence from the poem to support your answers.   (4 marks)
    (b) Explain why you agree or disagree with the poet's attitudes to those people.   (2 marks)

7. Choose **one** of the following themes and write down what you have learned about it from your reading of this poem.
    (a) physical disability;
    (b) the hypocrisy of the Church;
    (c) society's neglect of the poor.   (4 marks)

Critical Response Guide
Assisi by Norman MacCaig

Paragraph 1 — Introduction — include:
- title and poet's name;
- the main character and where the poet sees him;
- a description of the beggar, *in your own words.*

Paragraph 2 — Explain:
- how the poet's description of the beggar *makes him seem less than human.*
- Write down some words / phrases which the poet uses in verses 1 and 3 to describe the beggar and explain why you think each one has this effect.

Paragraph 3 — Include:
- your impression of the priest;
- quote from verse 2, explain / comment to support each point.

Paragraph 4 — Explain:
- to what MacCaig compares the priest and the tourists in the third verse of the poem;
- quote / explain / comment to support each point;
- what the poet is saying about the priest and the tourists in these lines.

Paragraph 5 — Explain:
- to what MacCaig compares the beggar's voice in the last 4 lines;
- quote / explain / comment on evidence to support each point;
- what he is saying about the beggar in those lines.

Paragraph 6 — Include:
- what you have learned, from your reading of this poem, about one or more of the themes of the poem.

Paragraph 7 — Conclusion — include:
- your feelings about the beggar and the way he is neglected by the priest and the tourists;
- some evidence from the poem to show that the poet feels like that too;
- one sentence giving your final impression of the poem.

VISITING HOUR

The hospital smell
combs my nostrils
as they go bobbing along
green and yellow corridors.

5   What seems a corpse
is trundled into a lift and vanishes
heavenward.

I will not feel, I will not
feel, until
10   I have to.

Nurses walk lightly, swiftly,
here and up and down and there,
their slender waists miraculously
carrying their burden
15   of so much pain, so
many deaths, their eyes
still clear after
so many farewells.

Ward 7. She lies
20   in a white cave of forgetfulness.
A withered hand
trembles on its stalk. Eyes move
behind eyelids too heavy
to raise. Into an arm wasted
25   of colour a glass fang is fixed,
not guzzling but giving.
And between her and me
distance shrinks till there is none left
but the distance of pain that neither she nor I
30   can cross.

She smiles a little at this
black figure in her white cave
who clumsily rises
in the round swimming waves of a bell
35   and dizzily goes off, growing fainter,
not smaller, leaving behind only
books that will not be read
and fruitless fruits.

Suggested Study Points
Visiting Hour by Norman MacCaig

Understanding

1. **The situation**
   - What is the situation in the poem? What is happening?

2. **The themes**
   - **At this stage in your reading of the poem**, what theme(s) have you noticed?
     (Don't expect to get all of them at this point!)
     Add to this list as you work through the poem.

Analysis

Verse 1, lines 1–4: Setting the scene: How does the poet help us to be there with him, in our minds?
   - Creating **mood / atmosphere**: Look closely at the way he describes his surroundings.
   - Consider what his choice of words tells us about how the poet is feeling in this situation.
   - Try to explain how each word / phrase achieves its effect.

   - **Synecdoche:** the poet mentions his *"nostrils / . . . bobbing along".*
   - What is strange about this statement?
   - What is the effect of describing his progress along the corridor in this way?

Verse 2, lines 5–7: Mood / atmosphere: continue discussion of **lexical choice** from **verse 1**.
   - Discuss the effect of the **enjambment** in lines 5–6 and lines 6–7.

Verse 3, lines 8–10
   - **Repetition:** the poet repeats the words, *"I will not feel".*
   - To whom do you think he may be saying those words and why?
   - How does the repetition add to the **atmosphere / mood**?

   - Can you see how the **rhythm** adds to the overall effect of this verse?

   - Explain how the remaining four words of the verse confirm your answers above.

Verse 4, lines 11–18: Mood / atmosphere: note details of the nurses' appearance, expression, etc.
   - **Syntax:** Comment on the word order in line 12, *"here and up and down and there".*
   - What effect does it achieve?
   - Also in line 12, what is the effect of linking the words with "and"?

   - What do these details tell us about the poet's attitude to the nurses?
   - What does he reveal about *himself* in his observations on the nurses?

   - Identify and comment on the effect of the **repetition** in lines 15–18.

Verse 5, lines 19 - 30
   - **Syntax:** Comment on the effect of the full stop in line 19: "Ward 7." *(This is not a sentence.)*
   - What is the effect of the poet's use of the numeral "7" instead of the word?

   - **Imagery / Metaphor:** There are many examples in this verse. Here is one to start you off: *"She lies, / in a cave of white forgetfulness."* (lines 19–20)

     (a) *The bed, screened off by a white curtain, in the centre of which she lies, **is compared to** a cave; it is a "cave **of forgetfulness**" because she is barely conscious.*

(b)   The metaphor is **appropriate** as she is cut off from the rest of the ward as effectively as if she were in a cave in the side of a cliff. The fact that the curtains are well above the level of her head adds to the cave impression. Because she is in a coma, she cannot communicate with the poet, nor he with her.

(c)   The poet is immediately aware that the patient is inaccessible to him, and he to her. "White" adds to the feeling of inaccessibility, as if the poet is seeing her through a white haze or snowstorm, a white-out or "white noise" which impedes communication. There are connotations of other cultures in the past where old people, when they became a burden, were left in caves in the hillside to die.

- Find other examples of **metaphor** in this verse and work out each example as above.
  (a)   Explain the comparison being made.
  (b)   How appropriate is the metaphor / image?
  (c)   What is the effect of the metaphor and (in some cases) of the connotations of the overall image being used?

- Comment on the effect of the **enjambment** in lines 29–30.

Verse 6, lines 31–38: How has the poet changed from the way he was at the beginning of the poem?

- Comment on the effectiveness of the following devices in this verse:
  metaphor, line 34; **synaesthesia**, line 34; **pun**, line 35; **paradox**, line 37; **oxymoron**, line 38; **alliteration**, line 38.

Looking over the whole poem
- Discuss the appropriateness of the **poetic form**.

- Look at the overall **structure** of the poem: Trace the *narrative* structure.
- How does it help us to visualise the poet in the setting?
- How does the structure mirror the poet's feelings?

- What do you think the poet achieves by writing this poem in the **first person** ("I will not")?
- The viewpoint changes in the last stanza. Can you suggest a reason for this change?

- The poem is written in **stream of consciousness** style.
- Does this style affect the way you respond emotionally to the poet and his ordeal?

Evaluation

- Look over your completed list of themes dealt with in the poem.
- Some you may want to group together as different aspects of the same theme.
- Decide if there is one main theme or an order of priority.

- What have you understood about the poet's attitude to the theme(s) he has presented?
- To what extent do you sympathise with him? Perhaps you find him weak? Give reasons.

- Look back on the different ways the poet has conveyed his theme(s) / feelings to you.
- How effectively has he done so? Are some techniques more effective than others?

- Has this poem revealed to you anything new, made you think about an area of life you had not considered before, confirmed or changed your mind about any aspect of life?

- Any other comments you would like to make about the poem?

- **Write down** one sentence summing up your final opinion of the poem.

Read the poem again quietly, to yourself, enjoy it and see how much you have gained from close study.

Using Your Notes for Revision
Visiting Hour by Norman MacCaig

Understanding and Analysis

(Use these questions to help you revise important parts of the poem.)

1.   *(a)*   Summarise the experience which inspired this poem.
      (b)   Note, in more detail, how the poet has used this experience to convey his ideas about death and dying.

2.   **Look over your notes on Setting the Scene:**
      (a)   Note the details in lines 1–18, which help us to imagine the scene.
      (b)   How does the poet use sensory observation in lines 1–4?

3.   **Look over your notes on atmosphere / mood:**
      (a)   Revise the effectiveness of lexical choice and synecdoche in lines 1–4.
      (b)   Note the presentation of his reactions to what he sees in lines 5–7.
      (c)   Note effects of repetition, rhythm and layout in lines 8–10.
      (d)   Note his reaction to the nurses in lines 11–18.

4.   **Look over your notes on imagery in verse 5, lines 19–30:**
      (a)   Make sure you understand how the poet uses syntax in line 19 to show his reaction on arriving at the door of the ward.
      (b)   Revise the effectiveness of the imagery and metaphors in this verse.

5.   **Look over your notes on the last verse, lines 31–38:**
      (a)   Note the ways in which the poet has changed by this point.
      (b)   Revise the effectiveness of the devices / techniques used to show the changes in him.
      (You should have notes on metaphor, synaesthesia, pun, paradox, oxymoron and alliteration.)

Evaluation

(You might like to practise for the exam by writing an answer to this question.)

6.   Discuss the extent to which you consider *Visiting Hour* to be an *effective* and *credible* portrayal of a person's reactions to such distressing personal circumstances as these, making clear whether or not the poet gained your sympathy.   (10 marks)

   *(Make sure that you cover **all** stages of the poet's ordeal, from entering to leaving the hospital. Consider the techniques / devices used to portray his reactions as well as structure and the style of writing used.)*

Using Your Notes for Revision
Visiting Hour by Norman MacCaig

Understanding and Analysis

(Use these questions to help you revise important parts of the poem.)

1. Write a few sentences explaining what the poem is about.

2.   *"The hospital smell*
             combs my nostrils
             as they go bobbing along"   lines 1–3
    (a) What do these lines tell you about the effect of the hospital smell on the poet?
    (b) Make sure you understand the words / phrases which make his feelings clear to you in those lines.

3.   *"What seems a* **corpse**
             is **trundled** *into a lift and* **vanishes**
             heavenward.*"*   lines 5–7
    (a) What do the words in bold above tell you about the poet's **mood** at this point?
    (b) Make sure you can give reasons for your answer.

4. *In verse 5, the poet finally reaches the ward where his relative lies.*

    (a)   *"Ward 7. She lies . . . "*   line 19
               What is the effect of the full stop after " Ward 7."?
    (b) Why does the poet write the numeral "7" instead of the word "seven"?

5. **Look over your notes on imagery in verse 5:**
    Revise your notes on the effectiveness of the following images:
    (a) the cave;   (b) the flower;   (c) the vampire.

Evaluation

(You might like to practise for the exam by writing answers to these questions.)

6. **Look again at verses 5 and 6, from "Ward 7 . . ." to the end of the poem.**
    (a) Write about the poet's feelings in this section of the poem.   (2 marks)
    (b) Refer to some evidence from the poem to support your answer.   (2 marks)
    (c) Explain, in detail, your own feelings on reading this part of the poem.   (2 marks)

7. Choose **one** of the following themes and write down what you have learned about it from your reading of this poem:
    (a) death;
    (b) love;
    (c) pain;
    (d) facing up to difficult situations.
    You should refer to the poem in your answer.   (4 marks)

Critical Response Guide
Visiting Hour by Norman MacCaig

Paragraph 1 — Introduction — include:
- title and poet's name;

- a few sentences explaining what the poem is about.

Paragraph 2 — Explain:
- how the poet feels about his *surroundings*;
- quote at least *two* pieces of evidence from the first three verses to support your answer;

- how each piece of evidence makes the poet's feelings clear.

Paragraph 3 — Include:
- how the poet feels when he finally reaches the ward where his relative lies;

- how the poet's feelings are made clear to you in line 19;
- quotations to support each statement.

Paragraph 4 — Include:
- what the poet sees when he enters the ward;

- details, as far as possible *in your own words*, which the poet gives in verse 5, to help you build up a picture of:
  (a) a hospital ward, and
  (b) a very sick patient.

Paragraph 5: Look again at verses 5 and 6, from "Ward 7 . . ." to the end. Explain:
- one or more of the following images: *(a)* the cave; *(b)* the flower; *(c)* the vampire;
- comment on the effect of the image(s);

- in detail, *your* feelings on reading this part of the poem;

- why particular parts of those verses made you feel this way.

Paragraph 6 — Conclusion — include:
- what you have learned about *death* and *dying* from your reading of this poem;

- how the poem, or parts of the poem, helped you to understand those themes;

- one sentence summing up your final impression of the poem.

HOTEL ROOM, 12th FLOOR

This morning I watched from here
a helicopter skirting like a damaged insect
the Empire State Building, that
jumbo size dentist's drill, and landing
5   on the roof of the PanAm skyscraper.
But now midnight has come in
from foreign places. Its uncivilised darkness
is shot at by a million lit windows, all
ups and acrosses

10   But midnight is not
so easily defeated. I lie in bed, between
a radio and a television set, and hear
the wildest of warwhoops continually ululating through
the glittering canyons and gulches —
15   police cars and ambulances racing
to the broken bones, the harsh screaming
from coldwater flats, the blood
glazed on sidewalks.

The frontier is never
20   somewhere else. And no stockades
can keep the midnight out.

Unseen Textual Analysis
Hotel Room, 12th Floor by Norman MacCaig

All answers should be supported by close reference to the text.

The poet is in a New York hotel room. He describes the sights and sounds in the streets outside his window.

1.   Referring closely to verse 1, lines 1–9, show how the poet creates
    (a) a sense of *time*, and   (1) U
    (b) a sense of *place.*   (1) U
    (c) Explain how the setting contributes to the mood of the poem.   (2) A

2.   *"a helicopter skirting like a damaged insect*
          the Empire State Building, that
          jumbo size dentist's drill, . . ."   lines 2–4
    (a) Explain the effectiveness of the simile in line 2 and of the metaphor in line 4, making clear what, together, they reveal of the poet's reaction and attitude to the Empire State Building.   (4) A

    (b) Consider the common theme in these two devices, and show how they form an effective introduction to a main concern of the poem.   (2) A

    (c)   *". . . a million lit windows, all*
          ups and acrosses"   lines 8–9
    Explain how this image adds to the theme in lines 2–4.   (2) A

3.   *"the wildest of warwhoops continually ululating through*
          the glittering canyons and gulches"   lines 13–14
    (a) Referring closely to lines 13–14, show how the poet uses Wild West imagery to take his argument forward.   (3) A
    (b) How does the poet's situation / position at this point in the poem add to the effectiveness of this imagery?   (1) A

4.   *". . . the broken bones, the harsh screaming*
          from coldwater flats, the blood
          glazed on sidewalks."   lines 16–18
    Show how the device, which the poet uses in these lines, serves to illustrate the truth of his argument.   (4) A

5.   To what extent do you consider the last three-line verse to be an effective conclusion to the poem? Justify your answer with reference to the whole poem but do not treat in detail any points already used in earlier answers.
    (You may wish to refer to such areas as structure, imagery and narrative stance.)

        (10) E

                       Total Marks   **(30)**

Unseen Textual Analysis
Hotel Room, 12th Floor by Norman MacCaig

The poet is in a New York hotel room. He describes the sights and sounds in the streets outside his window.

1. Write down the following, giving *two* pieces of evidence from the poem for each one:
   - (a) the time of day **when the poem is being written**;   (2) U
   - (b) the place (inside) where the poet is;   (2) U
   - (c) the place (outside) where the poet is.   (2) U

2. (a) Write down a *phrase* from verse 1, which describes the Empire State Building.   (2) U
   - (b) Explain how this phrase lets you know what the poet thinks of the Empire State Building.   (2) A

3.
   > *"a helicopter skirting like a damaged insect*
   > *the Empire State Building"*   lines 2–3
   - (a) To what does the poet compare the helicopter in these lines?   (1) U
   - (b) Write down *two* ways in which those two things are alike.   (2) A
   - (c) How does this comparison help us to appreciate the height of the Empire State Building?   (1) A

4.
   > *"the wildest of warwhoops continually ululating . . ."* line 13
   - (a) Name two sources of the **sounds**, which the poet hears outside.   (2) U
   - (b) Write down *two* words from line 13 above, which help you to imagine what those sounds are like.   (2) A
   - (c) What do you think the poet wants these words to remind you of?   (1) A
   - (d) Try to explain why this is a good way to describe those sounds.   (2) A

5.
   > *". . . the broken bones, the harsh screaming*
   > *from coldwater flats, the blood*
   > *glazed on the sidewalks."*   lines 16–18
   - (a) What is the poet concerned about in these lines?   (2) U
   - (b) How do you think the poet feels about the situation described here?   (2) A

6. *The poet gives us a vivid description of life in New York.*
   - Write about some of the things he mentions, which you find particularly *sad* or *frightening* or which *make you think about some aspect of life*, trying to explain why they have this effect on you.

   (You may deal with any one or more of these areas.)   (5) E

   Total Marks   (30)

Suggestions for Critical Essays

(For general guidance on writing critical essays, see page 165.)

1. A poem is often inspired by an intense emotional experience.
   Choose one such poem and examine the techniques used by the poet to convey the significance of the experience or event which gave rise to the poem.

   [This question is suitable for any one of the poems in this chapter.]
   Use your discussion notes.

2. Select a poem, which has genuinely shocked you.
   Explain which aspects of the poet's ideas and of the devices he uses, provoked this strong response in you.

   [This poem is suitable for *Assisi* or, if you have studied the unseen poem, *Hotel Room, 12th Floor.*]
   Use your discussion notes.

3. Choose a poem in which the poet's feelings are revealed.
   By close reference to the poem, explain how the literary and linguistic techniques, used by the poet, help to convey the theme(s) and the extent to which the poet was successful in engaging your sympathy.

   [This question is suitable for either of the poems discussed in this chapter.]
   Use your discussion notes.

4. Compare and contrast two poems by the same writer and, by close reference to the techniques / devices used in both poems, explain which, in your opinion, has put across the stronger message.

   [This question is suitable for a comparison / contrast between *Assisi* and *Visiting Hour*, or, if you have studied the unseen poem, *Assisi* and *Hotel Room, 12th Floor.*]
   Use your discussion notes.

Some Ideas and Suggestions for Writing

(For general guidance on writing essays for the Language Study unit, see page 168.)

1.   **Write about an aspect of our society that shocks you.**
     Explain what you think society or the government should be doing to help.
     (This can be done as expressive writing: a **persuasive essay**; or as a **Report**.)
     There are plenty of possibilities here; choose one you have researched or which you know about personally: e.g., homelessness, abortion, drugs, street violence, student fees . . . By all means use research from another subject like Modern Studies, in which case it would come into the Report category, but it will also have to comply with the arrangements for English and should concentrate on the facts and take an objective stance. You should also consider the purpose of the report, e.g., magazine article, government enquiry . . . Alternatively, it could be done on a more personal level, as a persuasive essay, still using the facts you have amassed but also conveying your feelings of shock, which should pervade the whole essay and be clear through your lexical choice, comparisons, etc.

2.   **Write about a time when you have visited a close friend or relative who was very ill in hospital.**
     (This is expressive writing: a **personal reflective** essay.)
     Try to convey the atmosphere of the hospital as well as your feelings before, during and after the visit. Did you cope well with the situation? Could / should you have done anything differently? Reflect on the effect this visit had on you — did it change your attitude to life in any way? Any other thoughts you have about the experience.

3.   **If you have or have had close contact with someone who is severely disabled, write about that person's life and how he or she copes with the disability.**
     (This is expressive writing: a **personal reflective** essay.)
     Explain the part you play in this person's life, reflect on such aspects as the apparent injustice of fate which makes one person able-bodied and the next disabled; the way we abuse our bodies and take our faculties for granted . . . any other reflections on the subject of disability / fate.

4.   **Write a short story in which a disabled person overcomes his / her physical weakness in order to achieve a lifetime's ambition.**
     (This is creative writing: a piece of **prose fiction** or a **dramatic script**.)
     If you choose the prose option, you may write from the point of view of the disabled person or as a detached observer. Try to show the disabled person as normal in other ways, not necessarily a saint!

5.   **Write a short story or a dramatic script set in a hospital, in which relatives are waiting for news of a very sick person.**
     (This is creative writing: either a piece of **prose fiction** or a **dramatic script**.)
     Do not spend time on the illness/accident; concentrate on the atmosphere of the hospital waiting room and the thoughts of, and tensions, past and / or present, between the waiting relatives. If you choose the dramatic option, you may like to consider a monologue or soliloquy based on the thoughts of one of the relatives.

CHAPTER 7
Edwin Morgan

The Starlings in George Square and *Trio*

EDWIN MORGAN, born 1920

The poet and his work

Edwin Morgan, like Norman MacCaig, is a city poet, but at the other end of the M8 from MacCaig. Born in Glasgow, he studied at Glasgow University, where he went on to teach for many years in the English Department. But Morgan is not a stay-at-home poet: he has travelled widely, lecturing in other European universities. He is very much an academic, but no ivory tower dweller: his poems reflect his great interest in human beings from all walks of life and have often been sparked off by chance encounters in the streets of Glasgow (like *Trio*, the second poem in the chapter), or inspired by someone he has noticed from the top of a bus, a brief newspaper headline . . . in short, his source material is humanity, past, present or future, with occasional sallies into the animal kingdom.

Morgan's Glasgow poems are central to his work but, in fact, make up a very small proportion of this prolific poet's output. In an interview reported in *The Observer* in April, 1989, he said, *"I like the sense of a contrast in Glasgow; it's a bizarre kind of place. Interesting and strange things are always happening."* Many of his Glasgow poems are heartrendingly sad, like *Glasgow Green*, which deals with a sleazy, homosexual encounter; others are hilariously funny, like the first poem in this chapter, *The Starlings in George Square*, which deals with a plague of starlings in the city, a very real problem in Glasgow in the 1960s, but Morgan tackles it in a most entertaining way, while still making a serious point. In the 1970s, he wrote his Glasgow Sonnets, a series of ten poems in sonnet form about Glasgow at this time of high unemployment with the loss of ship-building and other heavy industry, and poor housing in the city, when the slum clearance programme was just beginning. Those poems capture the essence of the old Glasgow. The heroes of some of his poems may appear on the surface to be "sad cases" but, for Morgan, they are survivors like the disabled man in that almost standard poem in Scottish schools, *In the Snack Bar*, and demonstrate the poet's faith in and hope for humanity, ideas which underlie much of his work.

Another theme which crops up in many of his poems is the problem of communication, one of the themes dealt with in *Starlings*. Addressing sixth year pupils in Langside College in October, 1996, he said, *"I like the idea that we might be surrounded by messages which we perhaps ought to be trying to interpret."* He touches on this idea in *Starlings*, line 66, and deals with this theme also in some of his experimental poetry, notably in *The First Men on Mercury*, in which he invents words for the speech of the Mercurians; by the end of the poem, as the space explorers are sent packing by the Mercurians, who are afraid the Earthmen are bringing their nuclear problems with them, the two sides have more or less exchanged languages. In the unseen poem in this chapter, it is the aliens who are rejected from Earth; in this poem he uses the concept of time travel, while teleportation is used in *In Sobieski's Shield*; in both poems, as in most of his space poems, he uses those ideas to throw light on fundamental human behaviour and emotions.

Communication is of course the poet's *métier* and Edwin Morgan is a master of his art, effortlessly reaching his audience, reading or listening, fifth year school students or the cream of academia. He continues to write, lecture and read his work to the public, a very youthful 78-year-old, who will, it is to be hoped, go on entertaining and giving us the benefits of his insight for many years to come.

THE STARLINGS IN GEORGE SQUARE

I

Sundown on the high stonefields!
The darkening roofscape stirs —
thick — alive with starlings
gathered singing in the square —
5 like a shower of arrows they cross
the flash of a western window,
they bead the wires with jet,
they nestle preening by the lamps
and shine, sidling by the lamps
10 and sing, shining, they stir
homeward hurrying crowds.
A man looks up and points
smiling to his son beside him
wide-eyed at the clamour on those cliffs —
15 it sinks, shrills out in waves,
levels to a happy murmur,
scatters in swooping arcs,
a stab of confused sweetness
that pierces the boy like a story,
20 a story more than a song.
He will never forget that evening,
the silhouette of the roofs,
the starlings by the lamps.

II

The City Chambers are hopping mad.
25 Councillors with rubber plugs in their ears!
Secretaries closing windows!
Window-cleaners want protection and danger money.
The Lord Provost can't hear herself think, man.
What's that?
30 Lord Provost can't hear herself think.

At the General Post Office
The clerks write Three Pounds Starling in the
  savings-books.
Each telephone booth is like an aviary.
I tried to send a parcel to County Kerry but —
35 The cables to Cairo got fankled, sir.
What's that?
I said the cables to Cairo got fankled.

And as for the City Information Bureau—
I'm sorry I can't quite chirrup did you twit —
40 No I wanted to twee but perhaps you can't cheep —
Would you try once again, that's better, — sweet —
When's the last boat to Milngavie? Tweet?
What's that?
I said when's the last boat to Milngavie?

III

45 There is nothing for it now but scaffolding:
clamp it together, send for the bird-men,
Scarecrow Strip for the window-ledge landings,
Cameron's Repellent on the overhead wires.
Armour our pediments against eavesdroppers.
50 This is a human outpost. Save our statues.
Send back the jungle. And think of the joke:
as it says in the papers, It is very comical
to watch them alight on the plastic rollers
and take a tumble. So it doesn't kill them?
55 All right, so who's complaining? This isn't Peking
where they shoot the sparrows for hygiene and cash.
So we're all humanitarians, locked in our cliff-dwellings
encased in our repellent, guano-free and guilt-free.
The Lord Provost sings in her marble hacienda.
60 The Postmaster-General licks an audible stamp.
Sir Walter is vexed that his column's deserted.
I wonder if we really deserve starlings?
There is something to be said for these joyous messengers
that we repel in our indignant orderliness.
65 They lift up the eyes, they lighten the heart,
and some day we'll decipher that sweet frenzied whistling
as they wheel and settle along our hard roofs
and take those grey buttresses for home.
One thing we know they say, after their fashion.
70 They like the warm cliffs of man.

Suggested Study Points
The Starlings in George Square by Edwin Morgan

Understanding

1. **The situation**
   - What is the situation in the poem?

   - Note briefly what is dealt with in each section.

2. **The themes**
   - **At this stage in your reading of the poem**, what themes have you noticed?
   (Don't expect to get all of them at this point!)

   - Keep adding to this list as you work through the poem.

Analysis

§1: lines 1–23
   - What is the **tone** of line 1?
   - What time of day is it? What are "the high stonefields"?
   - Consider the **lexical choice** here: what do those words remind you of?

   - Discuss the **image** of the starlings presented in lines 2–4.

   - Identify and discuss the effectiveness of the **figure of speech** in line 5.
   - Discuss how the **imagery** used here was introduced in line 1 and is continued in line 6.

   - Identify and discuss the effectiveness of the **figure of speech** in line 7.

   - Discuss the **lexical choice** and the **layout** of the words in lines 8–10.
   - What is the effect of this manipulation of words and of the **repetition** in those lines?
   - What is the effect of the **alliteration** in line 11, and again in line 14?

   - In line 12, the poet uses a filming technique. What is it and what is its effect?
   - What is the child's reaction to the starlings? And that of his father?

   - Through whose eyes do we see in lines 15–23?
   - What is the effect of this technique? Which one of the themes does it help to convey?
   - How does the poet convey the **sound** made by the birds in those lines?
   - Discuss the **lexical choice** here.
   - What effect is created by the last 2 lines of this section?

§2: lines 24–44
   - What is dealt with in §2?
   - Discuss the change of **tone** in this section.
   - Discuss the **lexical choice** and its effects in this section.

   - Discuss the **humour** (visual and aural) in this section:
   - How is it created? What is its effect? Which one of the themes does it help to convey?

   - Consider the significance of the GPO and the City Information Bureau:
   - Discuss the effectiveness of the **simile** in line 33.
   - What is the effect of the gap between lines 37–38? What does it contribute to the theme?

§3: lines 45–70

- What does the poet deal with in lines 45–56?
- Discuss the **pun** on "eavesdroppers", line 49. What is its effect?
- What **tone** do you detect in those lines? How is the tone made clear to you?
- Discuss the effect of the **alliteration** in line 58.
- Discuss the poet's attitude revealed in those lines.

- In lines 62–70, the tone changes quite abruptly.
- Discuss the tone and the possible **ambiguity** in line 62.
- What attitude to the birds is revealed in those lines?
- Which themes are dealt with here?

- What is meant by "the warm cliffs of man" in line 70?
- How effective is line 70 as the final line of the poem?

Looking over the whole poem

- At which point in the poem do you detect the poet's own voice?

- Discuss the **poetic form** used in this poem. How appropriate is it?

- Discuss the effect created by the **juxtaposition** of the three sections.
- What contribution is made by the **style** of each section?

Evaluation

- Look over your completed list of themes dealt with in the poem.
- Some you may want to group together as different aspects of the same theme.
- Decide if there is one main theme or an order of priority.

- What have you understood about the poet's attitude to the theme(s) he has presented?
- To what extent do you agree or disagree with him? Give reasons.

- Look back on the different ways the poet has conveyed his theme(s) / attitudes to you.
- How effectively has he done so? Are some techniques more effective than others?

- How successfully has the poet created a sense of place in this poem?

- Has this poem revealed to you anything new, made you think about an area of life you had not considered before, confirmed or changed your mind about any aspect of life?

- Any other comments you would like to make about the poem?

- **Write down** one sentence summing up your final opinion of the poem.

Read the poem again quietly, to yourself, enjoy it and see how much you have gained from close study.

Using Your Notes for Revision
The Starlings in George Square by Edwin Morgan

Understanding and Analysis

(Use these questions to help you to revise important parts of the poem.)

1.   *(a)*   Summarise what is dealt with in each of the three sections.
      (b)   What could a stranger learn from the poem about this area of the city and its citizens?

2.   **Look over your notes on section 1, lines 1–23:**
Revise the effectiveness of the devices / techniques which Morgan uses to describe the starlings.
(You should have notes on imagery, sound effects, lexical choice, repetition and alliteration.)

3.   **Look over your notes on section 2, lines 24–44:**
   (a)   Note the change of **tone** in this section.
   (b)   Identify the tone throughout this section.
   (c)   Revise the techniques / devices, which contribute to that tone.
(You should have notes on lexical choice, metonymy, hyperbole, repetition, simile and onomatopoeia.)

4.   **Look over your notes on section 3, lines 45–70:**
   (a)   Note the different solutions that were tried to get rid of the starlings.
   (b)   Note the further changes of tone in this section:

-   Identify the tone in lines 45–61.

-   Revise the techniques / devices, which contribute to that tone.
(You should have notes on irony, hyperbole and alliteration.)

-   Identify the tone in lines 62–70.

-   In what way is the tone of those lines different from that anywhere else in the poem?

Evaluation

(You might like to practise for the exam by writing an answer to this question.)

5.   What have you understood about Edwin Morgan's attitude to the starlings and to what extent has his presentation of the situation led you to agree or disagree with his view?   (10 marks)

     (You must decide at which point the poet's true voice can be heard. Consider, then, how you reacted to the different ways in which he presented the problem.)

Using Your Notes for Revision
The Starlings in George Square by Edwin Morgan

| **Understanding and Analysis** |

(Use these questions to help you revise important parts of the poem.)

1. *(a)* What is the poem about?
    (b) Explain briefly what is dealt with in each section.

2. **From reading this poem:**
    (a) What could a stranger learn about this area of the city?
    (b) What impression might a stranger form about the people of Glasgow?

3. **Look over your notes on section 1, lines 1–23:**
    (a) How does the poet create the impression of the *number* of birds in lines 2–3?
    (b) What aspect of the birds is he describing in *"like a shower of arrows"* in line 5?
    (c) Explain why this simile makes an effective comparison.
    (d) Explain the image used in line 7.
    (e) Why is this a good description of the birds?

4. **In lines 12–14, the poet mentions a man and his son:**
    (a) What is the boy's reaction to the birds?
    (b) Find the word in line 14 which makes this reaction clear.
    (c) Find the words used further down this section which show the same reaction.

5. **Look over your notes on section 2, lines 24–44:**
    What effect did the birds have on the people around George Square?

6. **In section 2, the poet uses a lot of "bird" words when he is writing about people:**
    (a) Revise those words and think of what he might have written instead.
    (b) What is he trying to convey to us by using those "bird" words?
    (c) What effect do those words have on the **tone** of this whole section?

7. **Look over your notes on section 3, lines 45–70:**
    (a) Note the different solutions that were tried to get rid of the starlings.
    (b) Revise your notes on the changes of tone in this section.
    (c) Revise the techniques which contribute to the tone.
    (You should have notes on irony, hyperbole, alliteration and ambiguity.)

| **Evaluation** |

(You might like to practise for the exam by writing an answer to this question.)

8. **In section 3, the poet mentions the methods used to try to get rid of the starlings:**
    (a) What solutions were tried?   (2 marks)
    (b) How do you think the poet feels about those attempts to get rid of the birds?   (2 marks)
    (c) Explain how the poet lets you know how he feels.   (2 marks)
    (d) To what extent do *you* agree or disagree with the poet's view?   (1 mark)
    (e) Which of the three sections of the poem helped you to make up your mind about the starlings? Explain why you chose this section.   (3 marks)

Critical Response Guide
The Starlings in George Square by Edwin Morgan

Paragraph 1 — Introduction:
- Title and poet's name
- Write a few sentences explaining what the poem is about.
- Explain briefly what is dealt with in each section.

Paragraph 2 — Explain:
- what a stranger could learn, from the poem, about this area of the city;
- what impression a stranger might form about the people of Glasgow.

Paragraph 3 — Discuss the poet's presentation of the starlings in section 1. Include:
- how he creates the impression of the *number* of birds in lines 2–3;
- what aspect of the birds he is describing in "like a shower of arrows" in line 5;
- why this **simile** makes an effective comparison.
- Explain: the **image** used in line 7;
- why this is a good description of the birds.

Paragraph 4 — In lines 12–14, the poet mentions a man and his son. Discuss:
- the boy's reaction to the birds;
- write down the word which makes this reaction clear.
- Write down the words used further down this section which confirm the boy's reaction.

Paragraph 5 — Include:
- a few sentences, *in your own words*, describing the effects of the birds on the people around George Square.
  Morgan uses some "bird" words when he is writing about people in this section:
- choose *three* examples of those words and say what you think he might have written instead.
- Explain: what he is trying to convey to us by using those "bird" words;
- the *effect* those words have on your reaction to this whole section.

Paragraph 6 — In Section 3, the poet mentions the methods used to try to get rid of the starlings — Explain:
- the different solutions which were tried;
- how you think the poet felt about those attempts to get rid of the birds;
- how you know the poet's attitude;
- the extent to which *you* agree or disagree with the poet's view;
- reasons for your opinions.

Paragraph 7 — Conclusion — Include:
- a few sentences summing up your final impression of the poem;
- whether you enjoyed reading the poem and why / why not.

TRIO

Coming up Buchanan Street, quickly, on a sharp winter evening
a young man and two girls, under the Christmas lights —
The young man carries a new guitar in his arms,
the girl on the inside carries a very young baby,
and the girl on the outside carries a chihuahua.
And the three of them are laughing, their breath rises
in a cloud of happiness, and as they pass
the boy says, "Wait till he sees this but!"
The chihuahua has a tiny Royal Stewart tartan coat like a teapot-holder,
the baby in its white shawl is all bright eyes and mouth like favours in a
                    fresh sweet cake,
the guitar swells out under its milky plastic cover, tied at the neck with
                    silver tinsel tape and a brisk sprig of mistletoe.
Orphean sprig! Melting baby! Warm chihuahua!
The vale of tears is powerless before you.
Whether Christ is born, or is not born, you
put paid to fate, it abdicates
                                        under the Christmas lights.

Monsters of the year
go blank, are scattered back,
can't bear this march of three.

— And the three have passed, vanished in the crowd
(yet not vanished, for in their arms they wind
the life of men and beasts, and music,
laughter ringing them round like a guard)
at the end of this winter's day.

Suggested Study Points
Trio by Edwin Morgan

Understanding

1. **The situation**
   - What is the poem about?

2. **The themes**
   - **At this stage in your reading of the poem,** what themes have you noticed?
   (Don't expect to get all of them at this point!)

   - Keep adding to this list as you work through the poem.

Analysis

§1: lines 1–8
   - How does the poet establish where and when the encounter takes place?
   - Discuss the effect of the present tense here.
   - What is the significance of the "sharp winter evening"? *(Look for a contrast.)*

   - Line 2 introduces the characters: can you see an analogy here?
   - Consider the significance of their number, what they are carrying, and the Christmas lights.

   - Discuss the effectiveness of the **metaphor** in line 7.
   - What is the effect of the **direct speech** in line 8?

§2: lines 9–11: *Those lines expand the references above to what each is carrying.*
   - Look carefully at the adjectives: what do all three have in common?
   - Discuss the effectiveness of the **similes** in lines 9 and 10.
   - What other figure of speech can you identify in line 10? What is its effect?
   - Consider the significance of "milky" and "brisk" in line 11.
   - Discuss the effectiveness of the **alliteration** in line 11.

   - How appropriate is the **line layout** of this section?

§3: lines 12–19
   - Discuss the change in **register** adopted in line 12. What is the effect of this change?
   - Look at each pair of words individually. Discuss the effectiveness of the **lexical choice**.

   - What is meant by "The vale of tears" in line 13?
   - What kind of language is this? How appropriate is it here?
   - What is the poet saying in this line?

   - Discuss the point made in lines 14–16.
   - Discuss the **register** of the phrase "put paid to" in line 15. How appropriate is this register?
   - Discuss the significance in the use of lower case in "fate", usually written with a capital.
   - Consider the full significance of the word "abdicates" in line 15.
   - What is the effect of the line layout here?

- What does the poet mean by "Monsters of the year / go blank" in lines 17–18?

- Discuss the poet's choice of the word "march" in line 19.

§4: lines 20–24
- Why is there a dash at the beginning of line 20?
- What is the significance of this **grammatical form** here?
- Although differently indicated, the same form is used in lines 21–23: discuss its function.

- Discuss the effectiveness of the **repetition** from line 20–21.
- Discuss the point made in lines 21–22.
- What is the effect of linking the nouns with "and"?

- Discuss the effectiveness of the **simile** in line 23.
- What image does it conjure up in your mind?

- Discuss the **tone** of line 24.

Looking over the whole poem
- Discuss the **poetic form** used here. How appropriate is it?

- Can you see the **irony** of the analogy?

Evaluation

- Look over your completed list of themes dealt with in the poem.
- Some you may want to group together as different aspects of the same theme.
- Decide if there is one main theme or an order of priority.

- What have you understood about the poet's attitude to the theme(s) he has presented?
- To what extent do you agree or disagree with him? Give reasons.

- Look back on the different ways the poet has conveyed his theme(s) / attitudes to you.
- How effectively has he done so? Are some techniques more effective than others?

- Discuss the effectiveness of the poet's use of an everyday situation to convey a significant message.

- Has this poem revealed to you anything new, made you think about an area of life you had not considered before, confirmed or changed your mind about any aspect of life?

- Any other comments you would like to make about the poem?

- **Write down** one sentence summing up your final opinion of the poem.

Read the poem again quietly, to yourself, enjoy it and see how much you have gained from close study.

Using Your Notes for Revision
Trio by Edwin Morgan

Understanding and Analysis

(Use these questions to help you revise important parts of the poem.)

1. In his introduction in *Worlds*, Edwin Morgan writes:

    "I think of poetry as . . . a special way of recording moments and events."

    (a) Summarise the "moment" recorded in this poem.

    (b) Note the ways in which the poet makes the event real for us.

2. **Look over your notes on the characters in lines 1–8:**

    (a) Note who they are and what each is carrying.

    (b) Make sure you can explain the Christian analogy here.

3. **Look over your notes on lines 9–11:**

    Revise the effectiveness of the techniques / devices used by the poet in his description of what each person is carrying.

    (You should have notes on imagery, synecdoche, lexical choice and line layout.)

4. **Look over your notes on register in lines 12–19:**

    (a) Note the change of register which occurs at this point in the poem.

    (b) Explain how the change is made clear to you.

    (c) How appropriate is this change to the sense of the poem?

5. **Look over your notes on lines 20–24:**

    Consider how effective these lines are as a conclusion to the poem.

Evaluation

(You might like to practise for the exam by writing an answer to this question.)

6. How effectively has the poet conveyed his ideas about Christmas to you and to what extent do you agree or disagree with his views?   (10 marks)

    (As well as looking at the poet's creation of atmosphere, you will want to deal with the Christian analogy and the way Morgan uses it to put across his essentially Humanist ideas.)

Using Your Notes for Revision
Trio by Edwin Morgan

Understanding and Analysis

(Use these questions to help you revise important parts of the poem.)

1. *(a)* Describe, *in your own words*, what the poet saw in Buchanan Street.
   (b) How does the poet help us to imagine the scene and the people there?

2. **Look over your notes on lines 9–11, in which the poet describes what each person is carrying.**
   (a) *The chihuahua:*
      • What does he tell us about it?
      • Explain why the simile ("like a teapot-holder") is a good comparison.
   (b) *The baby:*
      • What does he tell us about it?
      • Find the simile used in the description of the baby.
      • Explain why this is a good comparison.
   (c) *The guitar:*
      • What does he tell us about it?
      • Why is it decorated?
      • How does the young man, carrying the guitar, feel about it?
      • Explain how you know this. *(Look at the poem before line 9.)*

3. **Make sure you can explain the Christian analogy used in the poem:**
   [Clue: three people, each carrying something at Christmas.]
   What other details in the poem support this idea?

4. **Look over your notes on lines 14–16:**
   > *"Whether Christ is born or not born, you*
   > *put paid to fate, it abdicates*
   >   *under the Christmas lights."* lines 14–16
   (a) Explain what the poet means by "you put paid to fate".
   (b) What point is he making in those lines?
   (c) Why does line 16 start so far across the page?

5 **Look over your notes on lines 20–24:**
   (a) Summarise what happens in those lines.
   (b) How good are those lines as an ending to the poem?

Evaluation

(You might like to practise for the exam by writing an answer to this question.)

6. *Edwin Morgan presents an unusual view of Christmas in this poem.*
   (a) In what way is it unusual? What is the more usual view?   (5 marks)
      (People usually complain that Christmas has lost its true religious meaning.)
   (b) Explain why you agree or disagree with the poet's view here.   (5 marks)

Critical Response Guide
Trio by Edwin Morgan

Paragraph 1 — Introduction — include:
- title and poet's name;
- what the poet saw in Buchanan Street;
- how the poet helps us to imagine the scene and the people there.

Paragraph 2 — the poet describes what each person is carrying — include:
- The chihuahua:
- what he tells us about it.
- why the simile ("like a teapot-holder") is a good comparison.

- The baby:
- what he tells us about it;
- the simile used in the description of the baby;
- why this is a good comparison.

- The guitar:
- what he tells us about it;
- why it is decorated;
- how the young man, carrying the guitar, feels about it;
- how you know this.

Paragraph 3 — Explain:
- what the poet wants us to think about when we read of those three people, all carrying something;
- other details in the poem which support this idea.

Paragraph 4 –   *"Whether Christ is born or not born, you*
                           put paid to fate, it abdicates
                                          under the Christmas lights."   lines 14–16

Explain:
- what the poet means by "you put paid to fate";
- the point is he making in those lines;
- why line 16 starts so far across the page.

Paragraph 5 — Edwin Morgan presents an unusual view of Christmas in this poem.
Explain:
- in what way the poet's view is unusual;
- the more usual view about giving presents, etc., at Christmas;
- why you agree or disagree with the poet's view here.
- One sentence summing up your final impression of the poem.

FROM THE DOMAIN OF ARNHEIM

And so that all these ages, these years
we cast behind us, like the smoke-clouds
dragged back into vacancy when the rocket springs —

The domain of Arnheim was all snow, but we were there.
5 We saw a yellow light thrown on the icefield
from the huts by the pines, and laughter came up
floating from a white corrie
miles away, clearly.
We moved on down, arm in arm.
10 I know you would have thought it was a dream
but we were there. And those were trumpets —
tremendous round the rocks —
while they were burning fires of trash and mammoth's bones.
They sang naked, and kissed in the smoke.
15 A child, or one of their animals, was crying.
Young men blew the ice crystals off their drums.
We came down among them, but of course
they could see nothing, on their time-scale.
Yet they sensed us, stopped, looked up — even into our eyes.
20 To them we were a displacement of the air,
a sudden chill, yet we had no power
over their fear. If one of them had been dying
he would have died. The crying
came from one just born: that was the cause
25 of the song. We saw it now. What had we stopped
but joy?
I know you felt
the same dismay, you gripped my arm, they were waiting
for what they knew of us to pass.
30 A sweating trumpeter took
a brand from the fire with a shout and threw it
where our bodies would have been —
we felt nothing but his courage.
And so they would deal with every imagined power
35 seen or unseen.
There are no gods in the domain of Arnheim.

We signalled to the ship; got back;
our lives and days returned to us, but
haunted by deeper souvenirs than any rocks or seeds.
40 From time the souvenirs are deeds.

Unseen Textual Analysis
From the Domain of Arnheim by Edwin Morgan

In this poem, beings from another planet travel back in time and arrive at a small settlement on Earth during the Ice Age, when Man was at a primitive stage of development.

All answers should be supported by close reference to the text.

1. *(a)* Briefly outline the story told in the poem. (1) U
    (b) Show how the structure helps to make the narrative clear. (2) A

2. *". . . like the smoke clouds*
    dragged back into vacancy when the rocket springs" — lines 2–3
    (a) Comment on the effectiveness of the simile in lines 2–3. (2) A
    (b) Explain how the simile effectively encapsulates the nature of the visitors
    to the domain of Arnheim. (1) AU

3. From a close examination of the language and ideas in lines 5–25:
    (a) What can you deduce about the nature of the domain of Arnheim? (3) A
    (b) What impression does the poet give us of the people of Arnheim? (3) A

4. *(a)* Referring closely to lines 25 – 35, show how the poet contrasts the people
    of Arnheim with the visitors. (3) A
    (b) Which of the two groups does he appear most to admire? (1) A
    (Justify your answer.)

5. **Look carefully at lines 19–33:**
    (a) What is the narrative function of those lines? (2) A
    (b) Comment on the poet's skill in building up to and achieving this effect. (4) A

6. How effective do you find the last short section, lines 37–40, as a conclusion
    to the poem? (8) E

    (You might like to consider such aspects as structure, resolution of the narrative,
    theme.)

Total Marks **(30)**

Unseen Textual Analysis
From the Domain of Arnheim by Edwin Morgan

In this poem, beings from another planet travel back in time and arrive at a small settlement on Earth during the Ice Age, when Man was at a primitive stage of development.

1. *(a)* Who is speaking in the poem?   (1) U
    (b) Explain, *in your own words*, what is described in lines 1–3.   (2) U
    (c) Why is there a gap between lines 3 and 4?   (1) A
    (d) "... we were there." line 4: Where were they?   (1) U

2. *We are not told the reason for the aliens' visit to Earth.*
    Why might the poet want to keep this information from us at this point?   (2) A

3. *Lines 4 to 8 describe the domain of Arnheim:*
    (a) What kind of place is it?   (2) U
    (b) Write down the details which help you to picture what it is like there.   (2) UA

4. *Look at lines 11 to 16:*
    What do we learn about the people who live in the domain of Arnheim?   (2) U

5.   *"A child, or one of their animals, was crying"*   line 15
    (a) What does this line tell you about the *attitude* of the aliens to the earth
           people?   (2) A
    (b) Give a reason for your answer.   (2) A

6. *Look at lines 19 to 33:*
    (a) Explain, *in your own words*, what happens in those lines.   (2) U
    (b) Explain how the punctuation in line 19 helps to create tension.   (2) A
    (c) Why is this an important part of the story?   (2) A

7.   *"And so they would deal with every imagined power*
           seen or unseen.
           There are no gods on the domain of Arnheim."   lines 34–36
    What point is the poet making about human beings in these lines?   (2) A

8. *Look carefully at lines 37 to 40:*
    (a) Where are the aliens in those lines?   (1) U
    (b) What effect has their visit to Earth had on them?   (2) U
    (c) Explain how their reaction to what happened on Earth helps you to
           understand the ideas about mankind raised by the poet.   (2) E

                                                        Total Marks   **(30)**

Suggestions for Critical Essays

(For general guidance on writing critical essays, see page 165.)

1. Scottish poets often use humour or satire to deflate pomposity or simply to ridicule. By referring to one Scottish poem, show how effective you find the use of humour or satire or both.

    [This question is suitable for *The Starlings in George Square*.]
    Use your discussion notes.

2. It is often thought that poetry is solely about serious and sad subjects.
    Choose a poem which deals with a happy occasion or incident and write about the techniques which helped you both to appreciate the joy of the occasion and to understand the poet's message.

    [This question is suitable for *Trio*.]
    Use your discussion notes.

3. Choose a poem which either
    (a) communicates very strong feelings or *(b)* creates a mood of reflection and, by close analysis of the language of the poem, show how this has been achieved.

    [This question is suitable for either poem: *(a)* for *The Starlings in George Square* and *(b)* for *Trio*.]
    Use your discussion notes.

4. Choose **two** poems, which deal with the same subject matter. Explain briefly what the common theme is and, by analysing how the language in each poem helps to convey the poet's ideas, discuss which of the two poems puts its message across more strongly.

    [This question is suitable for a comparison between *Trio* and the unseen poem *From the Domain of Arnheim*, if you have studied the latter poem in detail; or, and perhaps better, for a comparison of *Trio* with *Lo! a Child is Born* by Hugh MacDiarmid, if you have studied that poem in chapter 2.]
    Use your discussion notes.

Some Ideas and Suggestions for Writing

(For general guidance on writing essays for Language Study unit, see page 168.)

1. **As a representative of an environmental / conservation group, write a report to the Government, putting forward the facts about the plight of an endangered species and requesting urgent action.**
    (This is **report** writing.)
    Choose a subject in which you are interested: it might be an animal, a bird, butterfly or any species which is becoming less common in this country or abroad.
    After introducing the subject, present your evidence of its increasing rarity. You should then think about such aspects as its natural habitat and why it is becoming rare. You might want to cover any action already taken to bring the problem to the public's notice and any steps taken to save the species. Close with a look at on-going action and perhaps a statement about why this species should not be allowed to die out.

2. **Write the letter which you might have sent to Glasgow City Council at the time of the starling "plague".**
    (This is expressive writing: a **persuasive** essay.)
    Decide on your standpoint: you will either be asking the Council to make a greater effort to get rid of the starlings, or you will be pleading with them to leave the birds alone.
    Whatever your attitude, you should express your strong feelings without being abusive.
    Set out your argument clearly and logically, justifying your request, in an attempt to win the Council over to your point of view. Choose your words carefully, using emotive language to affect the Council, as humane leaders of the people: stoop to flattery, if necessary, but don't overdo it or it will appear to be insincere.

3. **Write a piece reflecting on some everyday incident reported in the press.**
    (This is expressive writing: a **personal reflective** essay; or creative writing: a **poem** or set of poems.)
    Choose an item from the news which made a strong impression on you: e.g., an abandoned baby, a dog threatened with death because of some misdemeanour . . .
    Write a brief account of the incident and then go on to write, in more detail, reflecting perhaps on what might have led up to the incident, the thoughts provoked by it and how it has confirmed or changed your outlook or attitude to people or to life in general.

4. **Write a science fiction story in which aliens visit Earth, or human beings travel back or forward through time.**
    (This is creative writing: **prose fiction** or a **dramatic script**.)
    Choose this question only if you are familiar with science fiction writing, but do not simply regurgitate a plot you have read: there are many sci-fi fans among teachers!
    If you choose the time travel option, do not waste time getting into the time machine, etc. Start at an exciting part of the story, when your characters step out of the machine or come face to face with an inhabitant of the time / place they are visiting. You will therefore have to decide where and when they are going before you begin. You can make it more interesting by thinking of a reason for their choice . . . to visit an ancestor, a great event or simply travel forward a few months to see what happens when the Millennium Bug strikes . . .
    Your conclusion should show that the characters have been affected in some way by their experience.

CHAPTER 8
Liz Lochhead:
Revelation and *Box Room*

LIZ LOCHHEAD, born 1947

The poet and her work:

Born in Motherwell in 1947, Liz Lochhead is the youngest of the poets covered in this book. Like Edwin Morgan, she is based in Glasgow but travels all over Great Britain reading her work. She studied at Glasgow School of Art and went on to teach Art in Glasgow for eight years. Her first collection of poetry, *Memo for Spring*, was published by Reprographia in 1972. She turned to writing full time when she was awarded writers' bursaries by The Scottish Arts Council, The Arts Council of Great Britain and The Canada Council; she was the first holder of the Scottish / Canadian writers' exchange fellowship in 1978. Of the poems in this chapter, *Revelation* and *Box Room* are from her first collection; *An Abortion* is from *Dreaming Frankenstein*, published in 1984.

Liz Lochhead does not hide behind her poetry; the poet's voice comes through loud and clear in most of her work. Human relationships are central to her poetry. The only female poet in this book, many of her poems are presented from a woman's point of view, but any traces of feminism tend to be tinged with irony. She deals empathetically with the female condition but seems to be saying that some women are their own worst enemies. All three of the poems in this chapter deal with the uniquely female experience. *Revelation* and the unseen poem, *An Abortion*, show the fragility of the female in the face of the male threat to her vulnerability. The second poem, *Box Room*, deals with the prospective mother-in-law / daughter-in-law relationship and uses the kind of wry humour, together with puns and clichés often employed by stand-up comedians in mother-in-law jokes; underneath the superficial comic posturing, however, a serious issue is worked through, confirming that the female / mother-in-law relationship can be much more acrimonious and damaging to a marriage or prospective marriage than the male / mother-in-law one. Another of her poems, *My Rival's House*, from her collection, *The Grimm Sisters*, deals with the same relationship.

At first glance, some of Liz Lochhead's poems appear superficial, even lightweight, perhaps because of her use of clichés. Further examination, however, reveals that she uses this device almost as a symbol for the stereotyping which she is criticising. The word or phrase that forms the cliché contains an underlying truth which has become meaningless because of its overuse; she is asking us to re-examine and react to the original impact of the idea contained in the cliché. Her use of everyday language, too, is appropriate to the subjects of her poems, for the most part ordinary people doing ordinary things. Most of her poems are in standard Scots English but she does, at times, use the Glasgow dialect to great effect as in, for example, *Fetch On The First Of January*, from *Dreaming Frankenstein*. In her poem *The People's Poet* for Edwin Morgan, from the same collection, she describes his poems as "chocablock with life"; the phrase aptly describes her own poetry.

Liz Lochhead is a multi-talented writer, who has seen her plays and revues performed to great acclaim in recent years. It is to be hoped, however, that she has not deserted forever her poetic Muse.

REVELATION

I remember once being shown the black bull
when a child at the farm for eggs and milk.
They called him Bob — as though perhaps
you could reduce a monster
5　with the charm of a friendly name.
At the threshold of his outhouse, someone
held my hand and let me peer inside.
At first, only black
and the hot reek of him. Then he was immense,
10　his edges merging with the darkness, just
a big bulk and a roar to be really scared of,
a trampling, and a clanking tense with the chain's jerk.
His eyes swivelled in the great wedge of his tossed head.
He roared his rage. His nostrils gaped.

15　And in the yard outside,
oblivious hens picked their way about.
The faint and rather festive tinkling
behind the mellow stone and hasp was all they knew
of that Black Mass, straining at his chains.
20　I had always half-known he existed —
this antidote and Anti-Christ his anarchy
threatening the eggs, well-rounded, self-contained —
and the placidity of milk.

I ran, my pigtails thumping on my back in fear,
25　past the big boys in the farm lane
who pulled the wings from butterflies and
blew up frogs with straws.
Past thorned hedge and harried nest,
scared of the eggs shattering —
30　only my small and shaking hand on the jug's rim
in case the milk should spill.

Suggested Study Points
Revelation by Liz Lochhead

Understanding

1.   The situation
- Describe the incident which forms the basis of the poem.

2.   The themes
- **At this stage in your reading of the poem**, what themes have you noticed?
  (Don't expect to get all of them at this point!)
- Keep adding to this list as you work through the poem.

Analysis

Verse 1, lines 1–14
- *In the first two lines, we read about "the black bull" and "eggs and milk".*
- What do you think those two represent / symbolise?
- Keep those **symbols** in mind as you work through the poem.

- Explain the point being made in lines 3–5.
- Now consider that point in relation to the **symbols** you discussed in lines 1–2.
- Look for contrasting words in those lines to help you with the symbols.

- Do you see any significance in the word "threshold"?
- What is suggested by the fact that someone held her hand?

- *Lines 8–14 describe the bull through the eyes of the young girl:*
- How do those lines relate to lines 1–7?
- Which features of the bull does she notice?
- Why is her perception of him gradual?
- What else develops gradually with her perception?
- Discuss the **techniques** used to reveal the girl's feelings as she looks at the bull.
- Discuss the effectiveness of the phrase "the hot reek of him" in line 9.
- Identify and discuss the effectiveness of *three* **devices / techniques** in lines 11–12.
- How effective is line 14 as a conclusion to the first verse paragraph?

Verse 2, lines 15–23:
- Note and discuss all of the **contrasts** set up in this verse;

- look for contrasting words as well as ideas.

- Discuss the continued use of the **symbols** mentioned in verse 1.

- Identify and discuss the contribution made to the themes by **irony** in this verse.

- Discuss the effectiveness of other **linguistic** or **literary devices / techniques**.

- Summarise what this verse adds to the poem as a whole.

Verse 3, lines 24–31:
- Discuss the techniques used by the poet to reveal the girl's feelings in this verse.

- In what ways have the "big boys" replaced the bull in this verse?
- Discuss the **tone** in lines 26–27.
- What does it tell us about the girl's attitude to the boys?

- *Lines 28–31 describe the girl's retreat from the farm.*
- Discuss the **lexical choice** in those lines.
- Discuss the contribution made by the use of **symbols** here.
- How effective are those lines as a conclusion to the whole poem? *(Consider the poet's use of **irony** here.)*

Looking over the whole poem.
- How appropriate is the **poetic form** used in the poem?

- Discuss the **narrative structure** of the poem:
- consider the narrative function of each verse individually.

- Discuss the **dichotomy** between the child's viewpoint, remembered, and that of the remembering adult.
- Work out which is which in the poem: when do we see through the child's eyes and when do we hear the poet talking?

- Summarise the poet's use of **symbols**.

Evaluation

- Look over your completed list of themes dealt with in the poem.
- Some you may want to group together as different aspects of the same theme.
- Decide if there is one main theme or an order of priority.

- What have you understood about the poet's attitude to the theme(s) she has presented?
- To what extent do you agree or disagree with her? Give reasons.

- Look back on the different ways the poet has conveyed her theme(s) / attitudes to you.
- How effectively has she done so? Are some techniques more effective than others?

- Has this poem revealed to you anything new, made you think about an area of life you had not considered before, confirmed or changed your mind about any aspect of life?

- Any other comments you would like to make about the poem?

- **Write down** one sentence summing up your final opinion of the poem.

Read the poem again quietly, to yourself, enjoy it and see how much you have gained from close study.

Using Your Notes for Revision
Revelation by Liz Lochhead

Understanding and Analysis

(Use these questions to help you revise important parts of the poem.)

1.   *"I remember once . . ."*   (line 1)
Summarise the childhood memory recalled by the poet and explain the effect that the incident had on her.

2.   **Look over your notes on the bull in verse 1, lines 1–14:**
  (a)   Note the way the poet builds up your expectations of the bull in lines 1–7.
  (b)   How does the poet let us see the bull through the girl's eyes in lines 8–14?
  (c)   Revise the techniques / devices used by the poet in these lines to reveal the girl's reaction to the bull.
  (You should have notes on sensory impressions, synaesthesia, syntax, lexical choice, synecdoche, and alliteration.)

3.   **Look over your notes on contrast in verse 2, lines 15–23:**
  (a)   Note the immediate contrast with verse 1. Which word signals the contrast?
  (b)   Note and make sure you can explain all of the contrasts set up in this verse.
  (c)   How does this verse fit into the structure of the poem as a whole?

4.   **Look over your notes on symbols:**
  (a)   Make sure you understand the poet's use of male and female symbols.
  (b)   Find and explain the various words / phrases which she uses symbolically.

5.   **Look over your notes on "the big boys" in verse 3:**
  (a)   What does the poet accuse the "big boys" of doing in verse 3?
  (b)   What does this behaviour tell us about those boys?
  (c)   How do those actions connect the boys with the bull?

Evaluation

(You might like to practise for the exam by writing an answer to this question.)

6.   How effectively, in your opinion, has the poet used symbolism to make a statement about the female condition and to what extent do you agree with her ideas?   (10 marks)

  (You will be dealing mainly with the way the poet uses male and female symbols, but do not forget to take into account the tone of irony which underlies some of her words.)

Using Your Notes for Revision
Revelation by Liz Lochhead

Understanding and Analysis

(Use these questions to revise important parts of the poem.)

1.   *"I remember once . . ."* (line 1)
   - (a) Summarise the childhood incident recalled by the poet.
   - (b) Why do you think the poet remembers this incident so clearly?
   - (c) Explain why *Revelation* is a good title for the poem.

2. **Look over your notes on the bull in verse 1, lines 1–14:**
   - (a) Why does the poet think that the name "Bob" is unsuitable for a bull?
   - (b) Which two words in lines 3–5 tell us what the name "Bob" makes the poet think of?
   - (c) Find one word in those lines which tells us how she really felt about "Bob".

3.
   - (a) What is the girl's first impression of the bull?
   - (b) Which features of the bull does the girl mention in lines 11–12?
   - (c) What technique / device does the poet use in those lines to describe the bull?
     (Make sure you can explain the effect of the device.)
   - (d) How does the poet reveal the girl's feelings in this verse?

4. **Look over your notes on contrast in verse 2, lines 15–23:**
   - (a) In her description of the hens in lines 15–16, how does the poet contrast them with the bull?
   - (b) What does the poet refer to as "that Black Mass" in line 19?
   - (c) Make sure you understand why this is a good description.

5. **Look over your notes on symbols:**
   - (a) Make sure you understand the poet's use of male and female symbols.
   - (b) Find and explain the various words / phrases which she uses symbolically.

6. **Look over your notes on "the big boys" in verse 3:**
   - (a) What does the poet accuse the "big boys" of doing in verse 3?
   - (b) What does this behaviour tell us about those boys?
   - (c) How do those actions connect the boys with the bull?

Evaluation

(You might like to practise for the exam by writing an answer to this question.)

7. The poet uses the bulls and the hens as symbols:
   - (a) Write down what each symbolizes.   (2 marks)
   - (b) What other symbols does the poet use in the poem?   (2 marks)
   - (c) Explain how those symbols have helped you to understand what she is saying about the female condition and why you agree or disagree with her ideas.   (6 marks)

Critical Response Guide
Revelation by Liz Lochhead

Paragraph 1 — Introduction — include:
- title and poet's name;
- the childhood incident recalled by the poet;
- why the poet remembers this incident so clearly;
- why *Revelation* is a good title for the poem.

Paragraph 2 — Include: how the poet introduces the bull —
- why the poet thinks that the name "Bob" is unsuitable for a bull;
- the two words in lines 3–5 which tell us what the name "Bob" makes the poet think of;
- one word from those lines which tells us how she really felt about "Bob".

Paragraph 3 — Include:
- the girl's first impression of the bull;
- which features of the bull the girl mentions in lines 11–12;
- the technique / device which the poet uses in those lines to describe the bull;
  (**Quote and explain** the words / phrases used.)
- how the poet reveals the girl's feelings in this verse.

Paragraph 4 — Explain:
- how the poet, in her description of the hens in lines 15–16, contrasts them with the bull;
- what the poet refers to as "that Black Mass" in line 19;
- why this is a good description;
- what the bull would do if he got out of his shed.

Paragraph 5 — Include:
- what the girl is doing in the last verse, lines 24–31, and why;
- what the poet accuses the "big boys" of doing;
- what this behaviour tells us about those boys;
- how those actions connect the boys with the bull;
- the picture of the girl presented in this verse.

Paragraph 6 — Conclusion — explain:
- how the poet uses the bulls and the hens as symbols;
  (Write down what each symbolizes.)
- other symbols which the poet uses in the poem;
- how those symbols have helped you to understand the poet's ideas.
- Write one sentence summing up your final impression of the poem.

BOX ROOM

First the welcoming. Smiles all round. A space
For handshakes. Then she put me in my place —
(Oh, with concern for my comfort). 'This room
Was always his — when he comes home
5   It's here for him. Unless of course,' she said,
'He brings a Friend,' She smiled 'I hope the bed
Is soft enough? He'll make do tonight
In the lounge on the put-u-up. All right
for a night or two. Once or twice before
10   He's slept there. It'll all be fine I'm sure —
Next door if you want to wash your face.'
Leaving me 'peace to unpack' she goes. My weekend case
(Lightweight, glossy, made of some synthetic
Miracle) and I are left alone in her pathetic
15   Shrine to your lost boyhood. She must
Think she can brush off time with dust
From model aeroplanes. I laugh it off in self defence.
Who have come for a weekend to state my permanence.

Peace to unpack — but I found none
20   In this spare room which once contained you. (Dun-
Coloured walls, one small window which used to frame
Your old horizons). What can I blame
For my unrest, insomnia? Persistent fear
Elbows me, embedded deeply here
25   In an outgrown bed (Narrow, but no narrower
Than the single bed we sometimes share).
On every side you grin gilt edged from long-discarded selves
(But where do I fit into the picture?) Your bookshelves
Are crowded with previous prizes, a selection
30   Of plots grown thin. Your egg collection
Shatters me — that now you have no interest
In. (You just took one from each, you never wrecked a nest,
You said). Invited guest among abandoned objects, my position
Is precarious, closeted so — it's dark, your past a premonition
35   I can't close my eyes to, I shiver despite
The electric blanket and the deceptive mildness of the night.

Suggested Study Points
Box Room by Liz Lochhead

Understanding

1. **The situation**
   - Who is speaking in the poem?
   - What is the occasion?

2. **The themes**
   - **At this stage in your reading of the poem**, what themes have you noticed?
   (Don't expect to get all of them at this point!)
   - Keep adding to this list as you work through the poem.

Analysis

§1: lines 1–3
   - What is the **atmosphere** of the meeting described in lines 1–3?
   - What techniques does the poet use to convey the atmosphere?

   - Explain the **device** used in line 2.
   - What is the **tone** in lines 2–3? How is the tone made clear to you?

§2: lines 3–12
   - What is the effect of the direct speech in this section?

   - What is the hostess's **attitude** to her guest? How does the poet make this attitude clear?
   - Explain the **ambiguity** in line 10.
   - What can you deduce about the character of the hostess in this section?

   - What is the speaker's reaction to her hostess's words? How is her reaction made clear?

§3: lines 12–18
   - What is the **tone** of lines 12–14? How is that tone achieved?
   - Discuss the **ambiguity** of the words in brackets.

   - What is the **tone** in lines 14–15? How is that tone achieved?
   - Discuss the slight change in tone in lines 15–16.

   - Discuss the effectiveness of line 18 as the final line of the first verse.

§4: lines 19–26
   - What is the effect of repeating a phrase from verse 1 at the start of this verse?
   - Discuss the effectiveness of line 19 as the opening line of verse 2.

   - In what ways has the **tone** changed in this verse?
   - What is the purpose of the **brackets** in lines 20–22?

- Identify and discuss the effectiveness of the **devices** used in lines 23−25.
- What is the effect of the words in brackets in lines 25−26?

§5: lines 27−33
- Discuss the effectiveness of the poet's description of the pictures on the walls.
- How do the words in brackets relate to those pictures? Discuss the **tone** of those words.

- Discuss the **ambiguity** in her description of his books.
- Consider how the **alliteration** helps to convey the **tone** here.

- What is the **symbolic** significance of his egg collection?
- Discuss the effectiveness of the **lexical choice** here.
- Discuss the **ambiguity** in the words in brackets, lines 32−33.
- How does the position of the words "You said", line 33, affect the **tone**?

§6: lines 33−36
- Discuss the effectiveness of the syntax in line 33.
- Discuss the effectiveness of other devices / techniques used in lines 33−34.
- Comment on "closeted so", line 34, in relation to the title.
- Discuss the meaning of "your past a premonition / I can't close my eyes to" in lines 34−35.

- Discuss the **tone** of the last two lines of the poem.
- Consider the **lexical choice** here.

Looking over the whole poem
- Look closely at the **poetic form** used here.
- How appropriate is it to the sense of the poem?
- Consider the effects of the **rhyme** pattern and any variations.

Evaluation

- Look over your completed list of themes dealt with in the poem.
- Some you may want to group together as different aspects of the same theme.
- Decide if there is one main theme or an order of priority.

- What have you understood about the poet's attitude to the theme(s) she has presented?
- To what extent do you agree or disagree with her? Give reasons.

- Look back on the different ways the poet has conveyed her theme(s) / attitudes to you.
- How effectively has she done so? Are some techniques more effective than others?

- Consider the nature of the humour and how it contributes to the impact of the poem.

- Has this poem revealed to you anything new, made you think about an area of life you had not considered before, confirmed or changed your mind about any aspect of life?

- Any other comments you would like to make about the poem?

- **Write down** one sentence summing up your final opinion of the poem.

Read the poem again quietly, to yourself, enjoy it and see how much you have gained from close study.

Using Your Notes for Revision
Box Room by Liz Lochhead

Understanding and Analysis

(Use these questions to help you revise important parts of the poem.)

1. Refresh your memory of the main characters in the poem, the occasion and how the characters relate to each other.

2. **Look over your notes on verse 1, lines 1–18:**
    (a) The arrival, lines 1–3: what is the atmosphere of the first meeting, and how does the poet make this clear to you?
    (b) The first chat, lines 3–11: How does the poet convey the mother's attitude to her guest?
    (c) The guest's reaction, lines 12–18: Examine the tone of those lines and how it is conveyed to you.

3. **Look over your notes on humour in verse 1:**
    Note examples of the various ways in which the humorous tone is created.
    (You should have notes on pun, asides (brackets), rhyme and reductive humour.)

4. **Look over your notes on tone in verse 2, lines 19–26:**
    (a) How has the guest's tone changed at this point?
    (b) Note the gradual descent from total confidence at the end of verse 1 to fear in line 25.
    (c) Describe the box room of the title and revise the techniques / devices used by the poet to show the effects of this room on the guest.
    (You should have notes on personification, pun and syntax.)

5. **Look over your notes on the relics of the boyfriend's childhood in lines 27–33:**
    Note the techniques / devices used to show her growing doubts and feeling of vulnerability.
    (You should have notes on rhyme, syntax, enjambment, alliteration, ambiguity and paradox.)

6. **Look over your notes on the guest's feelings in lines 33–36:**
    Note the techniques / devices used to show her final descent into despair.
    (You should have notes on rhyme, syntax, enjambment, alliteration, ambiguity and paradox.)

Evaluation

(You might like to practise for the exam by writing an answer to this question.)

7. Discuss the part played by humour in the poem, explaining the extent to which this feature helped you to understand the speaker's personality and the ideas expressed in the poem.   (10 marks)

    (Think of the ways in which the guest tries to fight against her despair. To what extent does this attempt to see the humour in the situation and in her position indicate her strength of character?)

Using Your Notes for Revision
Box Room by Liz Lochhead

Understanding and Analysis

(Use these questions to help you revise important parts of the poem.)

1.   *(a)*   Who are the main characters in the poem?
      (b)   What is the occasion described here?
      (c)   How do the two women get on with each other?

2.   **Look over your notes on lines 1–3:**
      (a)   Describe the atmosphere in the first two lines.
      (b)   How does the punctuation help to convey the atmosphere?
      (c)   What is the speaker's tone in the words in brackets in line 3?

3.   **Look over your notes on lines 3–11:**
      (a)   What does the poet gain by using direct speech in those lines?
      (b)   What can we learn about the hostess's feelings from those lines?

4.   **Look over your notes on lines 12–18:**
      (a)   What are the younger woman's feelings after her hostess has gone?
      (b)   Pick out some words / phrases from lines 14–18 which help you to understand the speaker's feelings. *(Make sure you can explain each one.)*

5.   **Look over your notes on lines 19–26:**
Describe the room in which the speaker is to sleep.

6.   **Look over your notes on lines 27–33:**
      (a)   What relics of her boyfriend's childhood does she notice in the room?
      (b)   Revise the techniques / devices used by the poet to show the effect each item has on the young woman.

7.   **Look over your notes on lines 33–36:**
How does the poet let us know how the young woman is feeling now?

Evaluation

(You might like to practise for the exam by writing answers to these questions.)

8.   *(a)*   Explain briefly why the two women do not take to each other.   (2 marks)
      (b)   Whose side are you on: the older or the younger woman's?
         Explain, with reference to the poem, why you support her.   (2 marks)

9.   *(a)*   What is your impression of the speaker's personality?   (2 marks)
      (b)   Write down and explain some evidence from the poem which has helped you to understand what kind of person she is.   (2 marks)
      (c)   How do you think she will feel next morning? Give a reason.   (2 marks)

Critical Response Guide
Box Room by Liz Lochhead

Paragraph 1 — Introduction — include:
- title and poet's name;
- the *main characters* in the poem;
- the *occasion* described here;
- how the two women get on with each other.

Paragraph 2 — Describe and explain:
- the **atmosphere** in the first two lines;
- the **techniques** which the poet uses to convey the atmosphere;
- the speaker's **tone** in the words in brackets in line 3.

Paragraph 3 — Explain:
- what the poet gains by using **direct speech** in lines 3–11;
- what we can learn about the hostess's *feelings* from those lines;
- the younger woman's *feelings* after her hostess has gone;
- how some **words / phrases** from lines 14–18 help you to understand the speaker's feelings.

Paragraph 4 — Include:
- a description of the room in which the speaker is to sleep;
- the **objects** which she notices in the room.
- the **techniques / devices** used by the poet and how they show the effect which those objects have on the speaker.

Paragraph 5 — Explain:
- briefly, why the two women do not take to each other;
- whose side you are on: the older or the younger woman's;
- why you support this person.

Paragraph 6 — Conclusion — include:
- your impression of the speaker's personality;
- some *evidence* from the poem which has helped you to understand what kind of person she is;
- how you think she will feel next morning;
- a reason for your opinion;
- a last sentence or two giving your final impression of the whole poem.

AN ABORTION

The first inkling I had of the beast's agony
was the something not right
of her scrabbling, scrabbling
to still not quite find
5   all four feet.
Sunk again, her cow-tongue lolled
then spiked the sky, she rolled
great gape-mouth, neck distended
in a Guernica of distress.
10   That got through to me all right
behind glass as I was
a whole flat field away.
It took an emblem-bellow
to drag me from my labour
15   at the barbed words on my desk top.

Close to, green foam flecked her muzzle
and drizzled between the big bared brown teeth.
Spasms, strong, primeval
as the pulsing locomotion of some
20   terrible underwater creature,
rippled down her flank
and her groan was the more awesome
for being drier, no louder than a cough.
When she tried to rise again
25   I saw it.
Membrane wrapped, the head of a calf
hung out and the wrong-looking bundle
of a knuckle. Then her rope-tail dropped
and she fell back on it, steamrollering it
30   under her.

When the summoned men came,
buttoning blue coveralls over
the Sunday lunches and good-suit waistcoats,
the wound string around one man's knuckles
35   meant business and the
curt thank-you-very-much of the other
dismissed me.

Shamed voyeur, back at my notebooks again
my peeled eyes caught the quick hoick
40   of the string loop, the dead thing flopping
to the grass, the cow on her knees and
up again, the men leaving, one
laughing at some punchline.

The thing is this. Left alone,
45   that cow licking at those lollop limbs
which had not formed properly
with her long tongue,
that strong tongue
which is a match for thistles
50   and salt-lick coarse as pumice stone
tenderly over and over again at
what has come out of her and she is responsible for
as if she cannot believe it will not
come alive,
55   not if she licks long enough.

Outside she is still licking, licking
till in the blue dusk
the men in blue come back again
and she turns, goes quietly with them
60   as if they were policemen
and she knew exactly what she were guilty of.

Unseen Textual Analysis
An Abortion by Liz Lochhead

In this poem, the poet witnesses the distress of a cow giving birth to a dead calf, with the intervention of two men from the farm.

All answers should be supported by close reference to the text.

1. Explain, in detail, what happens in the poem and the part played in the incident by the poet. (2) U

2. By close reference to *two* language features in lines 1–5, show how the poet becomes aware of the cow's distress. (2) A

3. Comment fully on the effectiveness of any *three* of the following phrases / sentences, describing the beast's agony:
   (a) *"her cow-tongue lolled then spiked the sky"*   lines 6–7;
   (b) *"neck distended in a Guernica of distress"*   lines 8–9;
   (c) *"green foam flecked her muzzle and drizzled between the big bared brown teeth"*   lines 16–17;
   (d) *"Spasms, strong, primeval as the pulsing locomotion of some terrible underwater creature"*   lines 18–20. (6) A

4. **Look closely at lines 26–30.**
   Show how the language and syntax of those lines helps to establish the tone. (2) A

5. (a) From your reading of lines 31–37, what is your impression of the two men from the farm? (2) U
   (b) From an examination of the language in those lines, what can you deduce about their attitude to the cow? (2) A
   (c) Referring closely to relevant areas from the whole poem, show how the men's attitude to the cow contrasts with that of the poet. (4) A

6. How successful, in your opinion, is Liz Lochhead in conveying her ideas concerning the female condition and experience in this poem and to what extent do you agree with those ideas? (10) E

Total Marks **(30)**

Unseen Textual Analysis
An Abortion by Liz Lochhead

In this poem, the poet witnesses the distress of a cow giving birth to a dead calf, with the intervention of two men from the farm.

1. What does the poet witness in the field outside her house?   (1) U

2. *Read over verse 1 again.*
    (a) What is the first thing which makes the poet think that something may be wrong?   (1) U
    (b) Write down *one word* from the first few lines which tells us that this was just a slight feeling which the poet had at this time.   (1) A
    (c) Write down the *sentence* from further down the same verse which tells us the poet is now sure that something is wrong with the cow.   (1) A
    (d) What has the cow done to make the poet sure that she is in trouble?   (1) U

3. *Look closely at the description of the cow in lines 16–23.*
    (a) Note four details of the cow's suffering mentioned in those lines.   (2) U
    (b) Name or explain the *poetic device* used in line 18.   (1) A
    (c) Write down another example of this device in lines 16–23.   (1) A
    (d) Explain how this device helps you to understand the cow's suffering.   (1) A

4. (a) Write down the *simile* used in lines 18–20.   (1) A
    (b) What two things does the poet compare in those lines?   (1) A
    (c) What does this comparison tell us about the cow's suffering?   (1) A

5. (a) What do the men from the farm do to help the cow?   (1) U
    (b) How do the men treat the cow?
        (Give evidence to support your answer)   (2) A
    (c) Explain how their attitude is different from that of the poet.   (2) A

6. (a) What does the cow do after the men have gone?   (1) U
    (b) Why does she do this?   (1) U

7. (a) What happens to the cow at the end of the poem?   (1) U
    (b) What kind of people are sometimes referred to as "the men in blue"?   (1) U
    (c) Why does the poet use that phrase in line 58 to describe those men?   (2) A

8. (a) What do you think the poet is saying about what life is like for women in this poem?   (2) E
    (b) What do you think she is saying about men's attitudes to women?   (2) E
    (c) To what extent do you agree with what she is saying here?   (2) E

Total Marks   **(30)**

Suggestions for Critical Essays

(For general guidance on writing critical essays, see page 165.)

1.   Often a poem is inspired by an incident in the poet's everyday life.
     Show how the poet uses her experience and, by skilful use of poetic techniques / devices,
     makes it important to a wider readership.

     (This question is suitable for *Revelation.*)
     Use your discussion notes.

2.   In a successful dramatic monologue, the speaker's "voice" is an important element.
     Show how the linguistic and poetic techniques / devices used by the poet are effective in
     revealing the speaker's personality.

     (This question is suitable for *Box Room.*)
     Use your discussion notes.

3.   Choose a poem that either communicates very strong feelings or creates a mood of
     reflection and, by close analysis of the language of the poem, show how this has been
     achieved.

     (This question is suitable for *Revelation.*)
     Use your discussion notes.

4.   Poems are often written as a result of reflecting on an intense emotional experience or on
     a significant event. Examine the techniques used by the poet to convey the significance of
     an experience or event which gave rise to a poem.

     (This question is suitable for *Box Room.*)
     Use your discussion notes.

5.   Liz Lochhead is a poet with a recognisable "voice". Referring closely to more than one of
     her poems, discuss the recognisable features of her poetry and show how the poetic
     techniques / devices which she employs help you to understand what she has to say.

     (This question is suitable for all three poems in this chapter.)
     Use your discussion notes.

Some Ideas and Suggestions for Writing

(For general guidance on writing essays for Language Study unit, see page 168.)

1. **Reflect on an event or chance encounter which has proved significant in your life.**
    (This is expressive writing: a **personal reflective** essay.)
    Dispose of the event or encounter in your introductory paragraph.
    The rest of your essay will be taken up with reflecting on its significance.
    You might consider such aspects as chance — being, or not being, in a particular place at a particular time; later significance of apparently ordinary action / incident; what your life might have been without this incident. Fate: is there a guiding hand somewhere? Do we make our own fate, perhaps by some instinct of which we are unaware?
    End with a strong statement, perhaps whether your life is better or worse since the incident.

2. **Write an article for a magazine (for males if you are female, and vice versa) in which you discuss the male or female experience, from the point of view of your own gender.**
    (This is expressive writing: a **persuasive** essay; or creative writing: a **dramatic monologue / speech**.)
    Start by making a strong statement of your point of view in general terms.
    Proceed to examine evidence from various situations which supports your opinion.
    (Remember to prioritise, keeping your most forceful ideas to the end.)
    Look for a framework to give your essay a strong structure, e.g., taking examples from childhood, early years at school, later school days . . . or in different situations, e.g., in the home, in school, in work situations, in public places.
    The focus of your essay is your own gender experience but evidence does not need to be personal; in fact, seeing a general gender pattern is essential to your essay.

3. **To what extent does your bedroom reflect your character?**
    (This is expressive writing: a **personal reflective** essay.)
    Think about colour, style, arrangement . . . Think about the state of tidiness or chaos.
    Think about the objects in your room. Are there any remnants from your childhood?
    What would a stranger learn about you by looking at your bedroom?

4. **"The Child is father of the Man." (Wordsworth)**
    Write a debating speech arguing for or against the above motion.
    (This is expressive writing: a **persuasive** essay.)
    First, find out about debating procedure. Assemble your arguments and decide on the order, keeping your strongest to last. The motion does not restrict your research to male subjects.
    One way of dealing with this motion would be to research some great men and women from history to find out if there were any signs in their childhood of what they would become in later life, e.g., Hitler, Burns . . . Remember that you are looking for character traits in their childhood, not just that this or that person liked doing as a child what he / she later became famous for. You may find it easier to research within your family, in which case you would have to interview older members of the family: think about the kind of information you want and prepare a questionnaire.

SOME USEFUL DEFINITIONS

WARNING! There is no point in simply stating the name of a technique or device; you must be able to demonstrate its effect and what it contributes to the impact of the poem as a whole.

Address	A poem in the form of a speech addressed to some person, animal or object, present or not. [e.g., *To a Mouse*, page 10]
Allegory	A story in verse or prose, with a double meaning, which can be read and understood on two levels. [e.g., *To a Mouse,* page 12; *The Storm*, page 84]
Alliteration	The use of the same initial letter in two or more words in close proximity to create a particular effect, usually intensifying the sense of the words so connected. Sometimes the sound of the repeated initial letter adds to the effect. [e.g., *Assisi*, page 109]
Ambiguity	When a piece of language can be interpreted in more than one way; often used for humorous effect. [e.g., *Box Room*, page 151]
Analogy	An agreement or correspondence in certain respects between things which are otherwise different. [e.g., *The Horses*, page 61]
Anaphora	(pronounced ana`phora) A rhetorical device in which successive sentences or lines begin with the same word or phrase. [e.g., *Such a Parcel of Rogues in a Nation*, page 30, lines 1–3]
Anthropomorphism	Conception or representation of a God as having the form, personality or attributes of man. [e.g., *Lo! a Child is Born*, page 42, lines 18–19]
Antonomasia	A figure of speech in which an epithet or the name of an office or dignity is substituted for a proper name, e.g., *"The Bard"* for Shakespeare or Burns; and conversely, e.g., "a Casanova" for a womaniser; "a Hitler" for a tyrant. [e.g., in the second sense, *An Abortion*, page 156, line 9]
Apostrophe	A figure of speech in which a thing, a place, an abstract quality, an idea, a dead or absent person, is addressed as if present and capable of understanding. [e.g.,*The Watergaw*, page 36]
Assonance	aka "vocalic rhyme" is the repetition of similar vowel sounds, usually close together, to create the effect of the sound of the particular vowel used, often with an harmonious effect. [e.g., *You Lived in Glasgow*, page 102, line 47]
Atmosphere	The mood and feeling, the intangible quality which appeals to sensory perception. [e.g., *Childhood*, page 55]
Caesura	(plural caesurae) A break or pause in a line of poetry, often marked by punctuation. [e.g., *Visiting Hour*, page 114, line 19]
Cliché	An idiom or figure of speech (often a metaphor or simile) which has lost its impact through being over-used. [e.g., *Box Room*, page 150, line 2]
Conceit	Juxtaposition of images / comparisons between very dissimilar objects, usually for the purpose of disparaging the "better" of the two objects. [e.g., *Hotel Room, 12th Floor*, page 120, line 4]

Contrast	Bringing two objects together to show the difference. [e.g., *Welcome to a Bastart Wean*, page 18; *Assisi,* page 110]
Dramatic Monologue	A poem in which there is one imaginary speaker (see Persona) addressing an imaginary audience. [e.g., *Holy Willie's Prayer,* page 22]
Enjambment	The continuation of the sense, without a pause, beyond the end of the line verse. [e.g., *Hamnavoe*, page 72; *Visiting Hour*, page 115]
Euphemism	The substitution of a mild and pleasant term for a harsh and blunt one, e.g., "to pass away" for "to die". [e.g., *The Old Women*, page 79]
Extended Metaphor	A metaphor which is continued through appropriate lexical choice over several lines, or sometimes through the whole poem. [e.g., *Assisi* page 110]
Form (Literary)	The genre, the kind of work, e.g., dramatic monologue, sonnet . . .
Form (Poetic)	The shape and structure of the text: rhyme and metre, as opposed to the substance or what it is about.
Hypallage	(pronounced hypa` llajy) aka **transferred epithet** Is a figure of speech in which the epithet, usually an adjective, is transferred from the appropriate noun to modify another to which it does not really belong. [e.g., *Holy Willie's Prayer*, page 24, line 47 "a lawless leg"]
Hyperbole	(hyper`boly) Exaggeration to emphasise the sense of the words; often used for satirical or humorous effect. [e.g., *Holy Willie's Prayer*, page 22, stanza 5; *The Starlings in George Square*, page 126, section 2]
Imagery	Figurative or descriptive language, often, but not necessarily, metaphorical to give heightened meaning, reveal feelings. [e.g., *Visiting Hour*, page 114, lines 19–26]
Irony	of situation, in which one seems to mock or to be mocked by Fate or the facts; [e.g., *Assisi,* page 109] or, verbal irony, in which the meaning is contrary to the words, e.g., "That was clever!" when someone has done something stupid. [e.g., *Revelation*, page 144, verse 2]
Juxtaposition	Bringing two ideas close together for literary effect, usually contrast. [e.g., *Assisi*, page 109, verse 1; *Hamnavoe*, page 73]
Lexical choice	aka **word choice**: The actual words chosen by the poet to create a particular or striking effect. [e.g., *Old Woman,* page 90, lines 1–4]
Litotes	A figure of speech which contains an understatement; the purpose is to emphasise the sense and the effect is almost ironic, e.g., "not bad!" meaning "excellent!" [e.g., *The Horses*, page 60, line 2, "put the world to sleep"]
Metaphor	A figure of speech in which a thing is spoken of as being that which it only resembles in some figurative (not literal) sense. When dealing with a metaphor, you must: *(a)* explain the comparison being made, what is being compared to what; *(b)* consider the points of comparison, what the two things have in common; *(c)* consider how appropriate the comparison is to the sense; *(d)* explain the effect of the metaphor — the point being made by comparing those two things; and, in some cases, the connotations of the overall image being used. [e.g., *Visiting Hour*, pages 115–116, lines 19–20]

Metonymy	A figure of speech in which the name of an attribute or thing is substituted for the thing itself. [e.g., *Such a Parcel of Rogues in a Nation*, page 30, line 13, "The English steel"]
Metre	The pattern of stressed and unstressed syllables in a regular verse form. Free Verse has no regular metrical pattern; it depends on natural speech rhythms.
Mood	Feelings of poet / narrator and / or the way the poet makes you feel when you read the poem. [e.g., *Old Woman*, page 90; *Visiting Hour* page 114, verse 1]
Onomatopoeia	A figure of speech in which the sound of the word reflects the sense. [e.g., *The Starlings in George Square*, page 126, lines 39–42]
Oxymoron	A figure of speech in which two words with opposite meanings are brought together to form a paradoxical phrase / statement. [e.g., *Visiting Hour*, page 114, line 38]
Paradox	An apparently self-contradictory statement. [e.g., *You Lived in Glasgow*, page 102, lines 20–21]
Pathetic Fallacy	A form of personification, in which an inanimate object is invested with human feelings, mirroring those of poet or speaker. [e.g., *Old Woman*, page 90, line 9]
Pun	A play on words which are alike or nearly alike in sound but different in meaning, often for comic effect but sometimes poignant. [e.g., *Childhood* page 54, line 15; *Box Room*, page 150, line 2]
Persona	An imaginary character speaking in a dramatic monologue. [e.g., *Holy Willie's Prayer*, page 22]
Personification:	The attribution of human qualities to inanimate objects. [e.g., *Lo! a Child is Born*, page 42, lines 1–5]
Register:	Particular form of language appropriate to a given situation. [e.g., *Holy Willie's Prayer*, page 22]
Repetition:	When a word or phrase is repeated to create a particular effect, usually to emphasise the idea contained in the words repeated. [e.g., *The Horses* , page 60, lines 15–20; *Lo! a Child is Born*, page 42]
Rhyme	Has two main functions: *(a)* aesthetic — it is pleasant to the ear, and an unexpected rhyme can provide a surprise, often humorous; *(b)* practical — it helps to organise the verse, intensifying the meaning, linking ideas by linking lines, concluding the sense.
Rhyme scheme	Is a method of denoting the pattern of rhymes in a stanza, usually represented by lower case letters, using *a* for line 1, *a* again for line 2 if it rhymes with line 1, otherwise *b*, and so on; e.g., in a six-line stanza, with lines 1 and 3, and lines 2 and 4, rhyming, followed by a rhyming couplet in lines 5 and 6, the rhyme scheme would be: *ababcc*.
Sarcasm	Language expressing scorn or contempt, often but not necessarily ironical; a jibe. [e.g., *Assisi,* page 109, lines 7–9; *Box Room*, page 150, lines 15–17]
Satire	A literary form designed to discredit and ridicule men, institutions and ideas. It is at all times some form of attack, fuelled by the poet's indignation. [e.g., *Holy Willie's Prayer*, page 22]

Simile	A figure of speech in which one thing is explicitly said to be like another with which it shares some characteristics; usually preceded by "like" or "as". When dealing with a simile, follow the same steps as those suggested under **metaphor** (see above). [e.g., *Lo! a Child is Born,* page 43, lines 16–17; *The Horses*, page 60, lines 25 and 37]
Stanza	A group of lines in a poem, forming a definite pattern of rhyme and metre throughout the poem. (Compare with **verse / verse paragraph**, see below.) [e.g., all of the Burns poems in chapter 1, *The Watergaw*, page 36, etc.]
Stream of Consciousness	aka **interior monologue**: A style of writing in which the poet appears to be writing as events are happening. [e.g., *Visiting Hour*, page 114]
Synecdoche	A figure of speech in which a part is used to refer to the whole. [e.g., *Visiting Hour*, page 114, line 3]
Symbolism	A symbol is an object, animate or inanimate, which represents something else, with which it has some connection. A literary symbol has the effect of combining an image with an idea. [e.g., *The Old Women*, page 78, line 12, "stones"; *Revelation*, page 144, line 2, "eggs and milk"]
Synaesthesia	Is the mixing of sensations; the concurrent appeal to more than one sense, e.g., "a heavy silence", "a hard voice", "a black look". [e.g., *Revelation*, page 144, line 9; *Visiting Hour*, page 114, line 34]
Syntax	The grammatical arrangement of words within their sentences. In poetry, the syntax is used to create a particular effect. [e.g., *Assisi*, page 108, line 20, "It was they who . . ."]
Tautology	Redundant words or ideas, e.g., "He was killed in a fatal road accident." A fatal accident is one in which the victim was killed, therefore "fatal" is redundant. Used for effect in poetry. [e.g., *Iolaire*, page 96, line 44, "tart sharp"]
Tone	The poet's or speaker's attitude to his subject, conveyed by the style of writing. Think of the tone of voice you would use if you were saying the words aloud. [e.g., *Holy Willie's Prayer,* page 23; *Old Woman*, page 90]
Verse	or **verse paragraph** is a group of lines which forms a unit in Free Verse, where there is no overall pattern of rhyme or metre. (Compare with **stanza**, see above.) [e.g., all of the poems in chapters 6, 7 and 8]
Zeugma	or **condensed sentence**, is a figure of speech, in which a verb or an adjective is applied to two nouns, though appropriate to only one of them; the verb is used figuratively in one case and literally in the other, e.g., "She threw a tantrum and a half brick." [e.g., *Hamnavoe*, page 72, line 27]

WRITING CRITICAL ESSAYS

The Requirements:

1. The criteria against which your critical essay will be assessed are the same as those for Textual Analysis:

   Understanding,
   Analysis,
   Evaluation,

   with an additional category: **Expression.**

2. No matter how the critical essay question is worded, you will always be asked to give a **detailed analysis** of the text, quoting, explaining and commenting on examples.

   - That does not mean, however, that it will be unnecessary to read the question, or, in the case of the critical essay part of the examination, that you can simply prepare your answer in advance, learn it up and spew it out in the exam; you will be asked to use your analysis of the text to prove something: that "something" is the important part of the question, and your answer must always be directed towards dealing with it.

3. **Expression** refers to the quality of the essay — how well it is written — in terms of its structure, style and language.

   - **Structure** will be dealt with in detail further down; it should show a clearly developed line of thought or argument, as you attempt to prove what was asked in the question.

   - **Style** should be fluent, communicating your meaning clearly.
   - Incorporate short **quotations** into a sentence.
   - Longer quotations should be on a separate line but should still fit into the sense of the surrounding explanation and comment.
   - Avoid quoting and then simply translating the quotation into different words; use the quotation to prove the point made.

   - **Language** should include the use of appropriate critical terminology. (See the section headed **Some Useful Definitions** on page 161.)
   - **Spelling**, **sentence construction** and **punctuation** should be reasonably accurate.

4. **Length**: Higher — minimum 650 words; Intermediate 2 — minimum 500 words.

Planning your essay:

- Points will be illustrated from the following question, number 1 on page 159:
  "Often a poem is inspired by an **incident** in the poet's everyday life.
  Show how the poet uses her experience and, **by skilful use of poetic techniques / devices**, makes it **important to a wider readership**."

1. **Read the question** carefully and **underline / highlight what you are being asked to prove**, e.g., in the question above, you are asked to show how the poet uses an incident in her own life to make a significant comment on something which is of universal importance.

2. **Introduction: (Understanding)**
    A short paragraph which should include:
    - the **title** of the text,

    - the **writer's name**, and

    - a reference to the **main point of the question**, in this case the incident and the area of universal importance on which the poet is commenting.

    - In other words, you are stating, in your first paragraph, what you intend to prove: but avoid the clumsy, non-literary "In this essay, I shall prove . . ." kind of introduction. Simply write something like this:
      "In her poem, *Revelation* (**title** of text), Liz Lochhead (**name of writer**) recalls an incident from her childhood, when she was taken to see a bull. She goes on to show that this incident, which marked her transition from innocence to experience, illustrates the vulnerability of the female in the face of male aggresion (**area of universal importance**)."

3. **The main body of your essay: (Analysis)**
    - This part will cover several paragraphs.

    - Make a reference to the question at the beginning of each paragraph, and sum up what you have proved in that paragraph at the end.

    - It should be possible to discern your line of thought or argument from a glance at the beginnings and ends of your paragraphs, e.g., "The incident clearly made a lasting impression on the child . . . (analysis of description and poet's reaction in first verse paragraph) . . . At the end of the first verse, the emotional impact of the experience on the poet reaches a climax with . . ."

    - Work through the poem, **quoting**, **explaining** and **commenting** on the poetic techniques / devices used by the poet.

    - Show how each technique / device contributes to the impact of the poem, helping you to understand the poet's ideas.

4. Concluding section: Evaluation

- You will have shown your response, at least implicitly, throughout the Analysis section; in this final part of your essay, you should respond explicitly to the ideas in the poem.

- This response should be directed to the main themes of the poem; the kind of things you have discussed in the Evaluation section of the Suggested Study Points:

- What you have understood about the poet's attitude to the theme(s) she has presented.
- The extent to which you agree or disagree with her, giving reasons.

- The different ways the poet has conveyed her theme(s) / attitudes to you.
- How effectively she has done so.
- Whether you found some techniques more effective than others.

- Whether this poem revealed to you anything new, made you think about an area of life you had not considered before, confirmed or changed your mind about any aspect of life.

- Any other relevant comments you would like to make about the poem.

- **End with** a few sentences, summing up your argument and making a clear reference to the question you have been answering.

Caveats (things to avoid):

1. Do not simply throw down everything you know about the text: all parts of your essay must be relevant to the question.

2. Do not simply tell what happens in the text and add a few comments. Include a **brief** summary of the situation so that the marker can understand your textual references. (Remember that external markers, unlike your class teacher or tutor, may not be familiar with the text; their experience allows them to mark your essay, however, provided you have set out your argument clearly and related each point to the ideas in the text.)

3. If you are relating the ideas in the text to your own experience, be careful not to depart too much from the text, by going off at a tangent and telling your own story in too much detail.

4. In the Analysis section, do not write a paragraph on each technique / device used by the writer; it is generally better to work through the poem, as you did in the Suggested Study Points: this way, your argument develops in the same way that the ideas in the text develop, so that the marker arrives at a coherent understanding of the poem and of your essay.

5. Do not forget the importance of the title: it can often give a clear indication of the main theme.

WRITING ESSAYS FOR THE LANGUAGE STUDY UNIT

The Requirements:

1. There are three main types of writing: Expressive, Creative and Report writing.

2. Within two of those main types, there are sub-types:
    Expressive: personal reflective,
                          persuasive,
                          argumentative.

    Creative: prose fiction,
                          poem /set of poems,
                          dramatic script.

3. Length for expressive pieces, prose fiction, drama and report: (H) 650–850 words; (Int. 2) 500–700; (Int. 1) 300–500; and (Acc. 3) minimum 100 words.
    There is no set length for poetry at any level, but the work should be fairly substantial.

EXPRESSIVE WRITING

General Advice:
- The structure of this kind of essay is very important in revealing a clear line of thought.
- Paragraphs should be well-constructed with topic sentences, developed clearly within each paragraph and a final sentence, summing up, and / or leading into the next paragraph.
- Paragraphs should be linked in a logical sequence as the line of thought is developed.

1.   Personal reflective:
- The essay will normally be based on a significant experience, which has prompted you to "philosophise", using this experience to reflect on larger issues.

- You should attempt to convey not only your conclusion / the effect of the experience on your attitudes or behaviour, but also the process of reflection which has led to it.

- Think about the tone of your essay, e.g., humorous, ironic; make sure that it is appropriate to the ideas you want to convey. Your lexical choice will be important in maintaining that tone.

- The reader should be able to form some assessment of your personality from your essay.

2.   Persuasive:
- Choose this type of essay only if the question offers something about which you feel very strongly and about which you are knowledgeable or willing to find out the facts.

- Your remit will be to persuade the reader to agree with your stated point of view.

- The tone of this type of essay can be anything from pleading to hectoring and all stages between those two. Use forceful, sometimes emotive language to maintain that tone.

3. **Argumentative:**
- You are required to present both sides of an argument in a clear and balanced way in this type of essay.

- You will present facts and opinions, without bias, on both sides; be sure to differentiate between those two: opinions can be disputed; facts cannot be altered to suit your case.

- Before you begin, you will know which side you favour; it is generally better to keep the best arguments for that side to the last, in order to lead smoothly into your conclusion.

- The tone of your essay should, at all times, be reasoning, informative, weighing up both sides of the argument before reaching an inevitable conclusion.

CREATIVE WRITING:

General advice:
- The two main areas of creative writing are content and expression.

- Look for an interesting way to convey the content to your reader, e.g., from an unusual point of view.
- Especially in a short story, you will not necessarily want to start at the beginning and narrate the story in chronological order: try using flashback, or withhold a vital piece of information from the reader in order to provide a surprise or shock ending. You can throw in occasional hints so that, in retrospect, the reader can see that the ending was in fact inevitable. (A good example of this type is *The Landlady* by Roald Dahl.)

- Try to use interesting and precise language in descriptive areas of your writing, including figurative language, comparisons and imagery.

1. **Prose fiction:**
- This can be a short story, an episode from a novel, a journal, letter . . .

- **Plot:** something has to happen, some sort of narrative development.
- There should always be a definite outcome to the narrative.
- You should always know how your story is going to end before you begin.
- It is not always desirable, however, to "spell out" the ending but it should be inevitable from the events leading up to it.

- **Characters:** Avoid having too many; two or three will do.
- Flesh your characters out in your mind, or, preferably, in your notes, before you begin, so that their reactions to the events in the narrative are consistent.
- Character can often be shown through effective use of direct speech but do not overdo it. Remember the restrictions on length: a page of meaningless dialogue, which does not either advance the narrative, or reveal character, is a waste of precious words. Dialogue can provide a good opportunity to use a dialect form to give your writing variety.
- Some conflict between characters or between character and narrative sets up the tension necessary for a good story.
- Some development of character in response to plot will help to give your writing substance and to convey your theme.

- **Setting:** a definite setting in time (past, present or future) and place (a small community, foreign country, an exotic location . . .) will help you to focus on interesting details, create atmosphere / mood, and, to some extent, determine the characters, language and outcome.

- **Theme:** sometimes the theme is what you will be given in the question; you have to construct a suitable narrative to illustrate the theme.

- **Structure:** keep the structure fairly tight; avoid rambling away from the point of the narrative. Advance planning is indispensable here.

2. **Poetry:**
    - This can be one substantial poem or a set of poems linked thematically.
    - **Do not regard poetry as an easy option because it is shorter than prose.**

    - Even if you are writing in Free Verse form, it is not simply a matter of chopping prose up into shorter lines. (Some poets appear to do just that, but they would not be given a good exam grade either!)

    - Poetry is a condensed form of writing: language is often used on more than one level of meaning; the connotation of words is important; and absolutely every word must work for you.

    - Arrangement of words is important and should form part of a sound or metrical pattern, which is relevant to the sense of the words.
    - Rhyme is usually better avoided, except by skilled practitioners.
    - Syntax can be used unconventionally; punctuation can be forgotten but it can often be used to convey an atmosphere, especially of tension, e.g., caesurae, short or non-sentences.

    - Try to use the techniques / devices you have studied in the work of established poets.

3. **A dramatic script:**
    - This may be a fully-developed play (within the length restrictions), a scene from a play, a monologue . . .

    - The advice given under prose fiction about plot, characters, setting and atmosphere / mood applies equally to drama.

    - At the heart of every piece of dramatic writing is conflict, as in prose fiction, between characters or between character and plot.

    - Most of your text will consist of **dialogue**.
    - Avoid communicating long chunks of narrative through a Narrator; you might just as well write prose fiction.
    - Dialogue should reflect the personality of the speaker. This is a good opportunity to show different speech forms. (SQA encourage use of the Scots language.) It should usually be possible to decide who said what even if the names of the speakers are not visible.
    - Dialogue should be natural, e.g., listen to people speaking and note how often they fail to finish a sentence, or break into each other's speech. It is important to keep the dialogue going at a reasonable pace, unless you are creating a particular atmosphere of discomfort, embarrassment, etc.

- You should also include directions to suggest movements, reactions, etc., technical effects and other production notes: your script should be capable of being produced by a stranger.
  - Such directions should be on a separate line, within square brackets . . . if using a word processor, choose a smaller point size or italic style.

REPORT WRITING

- The Report is a piece of writing based on information selected from material relevant to the subject, appropriately reorganised and expressed in your own words.

- The Report will usually be for a specified purpose and will be assessed for its effectiveness in fulfilling that purpose.

- Information should be drawn from at least four sources for an award at Higher level, three sources at Intermediate levels, and two sources at Access level.
  These might be from one or more of the following:
  - text books. reference books, newspaper / magazine articles among other print sources;
  - surveys using questionnaires, taped interview, etc.;
  - radio or television programmes;
  - the Internet.
  - **All sources must be acknowledged.**

- The Report must deal with complex ideas but it may be necessary to express those ideas in fairly simple language / structure, depending on the nature of the reader for whom the Report is being compiled. The target readership will be specified in the remit.

- Your persona! opinion is irrelevant in a Report; the task is to select information relevant to the specified remit from the available material. You may be asked to make specific recommendations: those should be based on conclusions drawn from, and your evaluation of, the available material.
  - The tone of the Report will generally be impersonal and formal.

- The Report should be clearly structured, well-linked, and information presented in a logical order.
  - Begin with a brief statement of the purpose of the Report and how the information was gathered.
  - Headings and division into numbered or lettered sections may be used.
  - Diagrams, tables, charts and graphs may be included if appropriate to the task.

- It is possible to use material from another subject, e.g., Modern Studies, but only if the preparation of this material complies with the requirements for assessment in English. Check with your teacher or lecturer that the subject, scope and purpose of your proposed Report are acceptable and that you have not had undue guidance in the other subject.

ALPHABETICAL INDEX OF TITLES

NOTES

NOTES

NOTES

ACKNOWLEDGEMENTS

We are extremely grateful to the following for permission to use copyright material in this book.

The Watergaw: Lo! a Child is Born: Wi' the Herring Fishers
from 'COMPLETE POEMS' by Hugh MacDiarmid.
Reprinted by permission of the Publisher, Carcanet Press Limited.

The Horses: Childhood: Horses
from 'COLLECTED POEMS 1921–1958' by Edwin Muir.
Reprinted by permission of the Publisher, Faber and Faber Ltd.

Hamnavoe: The Old Women: The Storm
from 'SELECTED POEMS' by George Mackay Brown.
Reprinted by permission of the Publisher, John Murray (Publishers) Ltd.

Old Woman: Iolaire: You Lived in Glasgow
from 'COLLECTED POEMS' by Iain Crichton Smith.
Reprinted by permission of the Publisher, Carcanet Press Limited.

Assisi: Hotel Room, 12th Floor: Visiting Hour
from 'COLLECTED POEMS' by Norman MacCaig
Reprinted by permission of the Publisher, Hogarth Press.

The Starlings in George Square: Trio: From the Domain of Arnheim
from 'SELECTED POEMS' by Edwin Morgan.
Reprinted by permission of the Publisher, Carcanet Press Limited.

Revelation: Box Room: An Abortion
from 'DREAMING FRANKENSTEIN' by Liz Lochhead.
Reprinted by permission of the Publisher, Polygon.

Picture of *Brutus,* Scotland's largest Clydesdale by Angela Catlin.
Reprinted by courtesy of *The Herald.*

Printed by Bell & Bain Ltd., Glasgow, Scotland.